THE LOVE ETHIC

THE LOVE ETHIC

THE REASON WHY YOU CAN'T FIND AND KEEP BEAUTIFUL BLACK LOVE

by

Kamau and Akilah Butler

Foreword by Chuck D of Public Enemy

CONTENTS

ACKNOWLEDGEMENTS

FOR your inspiration, support, or assistance in our lives and this project, Kamau and Akilah send special thanks out to:

The Creator for always having his hand on our lives.

Our parents and family who are the guiding force in our lives and always love us, no matter what the circumstance. We love you!

To our son, Jabari, the most wonderful little boy possible.

To Chuck D, who wrote the foreword of this book so magnificently and created the most significant Hip-Hop group of all time, Public Enemy.

To Jay, we love you dawg! You are the coolest cat.

To Anaya, for all your help with laying out the book and developing the website.

To Erica, Bobby, Dr. Charles Payne, Shanee, Tene, Natasha, Anthony, Joan, Phyllis, Dr. Achebe Toldson, Marshella, Jemell, Lisa, Derek, Woullard Lett, Malika Sanders, Dr. Jelani Mandara, Dr. Waldo Johnson, Phil, Eric, Laurie, Kelli, Patrick, and Delaina, your conversations and late-night talks formed the basis of this book.

To the late and great Dr. Edward Gaffney, Morehouse College professor of psychology, you were a giant of a man in character and deed. We know your essence touched this project.

To Baba Wekesa, who is quite possibly the most brilliant human being we have ever met.

Professor Naomi T. Ward, Dr. Sarita Davis, Professor Hattie Mitchell, Dr. Cedric Herring, for your educational guidance.

To Marimba Ani, Amos Wilson, Cornel West, Michael Eric Dyson, Patricia Hill Collins, Jawanza Kunjufu, Al Sharpton, Carter

G. Woodson, Martin Luther King Jr., Na'im Akbar, Greg Kamathi Carr, Wade Nobles, Bakari Kitwana, William C. Rhoden, John Henrik Clarke, Asa Hilliard, Jacob Caruthers, Joy Leary, Haki Madhubuti, Amira Baraka, Sonia Sanchez, Molefi Asante, Dorothy Roberts, Jerome Schiele, Earl Ofari Hutchinson, Claud Anderson, A.J. and Nancy Boyd Franklin, Malcolm X, Ray Winbush, Bell Hooks, Tony Browder, Bunseki Fu-Kau, and Ivan Van Sertima, your scholarship, writing, poetry, activism, creativity, and spirit have helped transform, educate, and liberate millions of Black people's lives, including ours. *Medasi* (thank you).

To Earl Graves and Susan Taylor who have created and guided intelligent, sophisticated, and informative media for African Americans.

To Aaron McGruder who created the *Boondocks*, some of the funniest and most intelligent analysis of Black people and American society ever. It really helped stimulate our thinking about this book.

To everyone who had anything to do with the HBO series, *The Wire*, HBO always seems to get it right with its original programming and documentaries. We watched the show throughout the creation of this text and enjoyed every innovative minute.

To Hip-Hop artists, Little Brother, Jean Grae, De La Soul, Just Us League, Joe Budden, the Roots and Joell Ortiz, and R&B artists, Chrisette Michelle, Jill Scott, and Erykah Badu, who create real, innovative, and beautiful music. Know that your stuff was bumping on the laptop while we were pounding out this book. You got us through. Keep moving, no matter what anybody says!

To the folks at Okay Player, you guys are an example that you can be true, authentic, and successful. Congrats! Continue to rep real hip-hop and R&B.

To you, the reader, who invested the time and energy to read our hard work. We hope it helps and enlightens you.

Finally, to anyone we left out, as Memphis Bleek would say, "Blame it on the head, not the heart!"

Peace!

To my parents, who made a decision to stay married and in love for thirty-six years and taught me the value of a solid and real relationship.

To my husband, Kamau, and my son, Jabari, whom I love very much.

Akilah Butler

To my mother, Norma E. Butler, who gave me love and life. To my teacher, Dr. Marimba Ani, who gave me love and knowledge. To my people, Jay, Eric, Phil, and Ashanti, who gave me love and friendship. To my wife, Akilah, who gives me love and happiness. To my son, Jabari, who gives me love and hope!

Kamau Butler

FOREWORD

By now, I have written many forewords for many books as well as a couple books myself, ranging from music to politics. However, when I was approached to write this foreword, my head and my heart were in two different places. I considered writing about Black love relationships as a difficult mountain to climb because Black love takes so many avenues. There are also so many different aspects to it.

I kept saying to myself that I was no expert in this category, considering I've had a couple marriages from my past that took similar paths, albeit in different ways. As a much-traveled adult playing music, I knew the strains of balancing lives, beliefs, and demands. Therefore, I compensated everywhere I could. I participated in family to the best of my ability through raising two beautiful daughters and a stepson as well. I was a reliable uncle and godfather for many nieces and nephews. Still, my relationship dilemmas were not manifested in my roles as a provider, partner, or even lover, but rather in continuity, togetherness, and unified thought. If only we could know who we choose ahead of time. Moreover, who says we make our best selections near our immediate space or while we're in our twenties and thirties? I certainly did not need anyone to raise me further. I was not looking for another mother or somebody with a daughter attitude for me to take care of either.

Nevertheless, I can't talk bad about either one of my past relationships, I am laid-back and try to make things work, but I definitely need the women in my life to be as complete a human being as possible. I have found that marriage requires this. I don't argue, and I have never agreed with it. I believe in equality in a relationship and think both parties should be as healthy as possible when coming into the union. This is the grown thing to do. Definitely, I have never been looking for a perfect person because I knew my life, situation, and schedule were never set in stone. I would say I thought I had it all figured out well by my second wife. We thought the same way. We were on the same path, and we had a similar way of relating to one another. We made everything work, or so I thought. We were two individuals thinking as one, working on being a lifelong couple. In the process though, I was blindsided by the fact she felt she lost herself while being with me. This, coupled with the joining of a very popular super church in the Atlanta area, hurled our paths in two opposite philosophical directions. I couldn't ever predict a split in our program. Up until that point, I actually thought I was made for being a husband. After that I wasn't too sure.

After our breakup, I went on traveling the earth and promised to keep my fatherhood duties above all. My philosophy was to be centered, but try not to marry again until it found me. I wasn't really looking for a girlfriend. However, love found me again, and I feel this relationship I have entered into in my early forties is as healthy as any I ever had. She is a great person from my hometown, and we are a great couple and good partners. For the first time, I am dealing with a person who has a strong father figure in her life. In my two previous marriages, I never had to deal with a father-in-law. This was new to me. Here was this person who was complete inside. She knew what she dug, and she shared my likes and dislikes. Her family was very tight, too. It kind of mirrored my family and the way I grew up. I knew my travel and lifestyle were going to be issues like before, but this time, I knew this great person had inner love and was connected solidly to her base (her family), so I knew we'd get through it.

I do not have clear answers for anybody else, but for me, this relationship showed me that there is something about familiarity that creates love. Every girlfriend or wife I have shared my life with, I have loved. I really tried to do this more for them than for myself. However, I knew there was another level. I knew there was someone who would match my effort and emotion tit for tat, a person who would come with the same amount of understanding and dutiful commitment I had.

I met my current wife, Dr. Gaye Theresa Johnson, in a chance situation of shared duty. I was not looking for it at all, but I was blessed by love finding us. Once love found us, we further built upon the gift by merging our dual lives philosophically upon the power of love and what we can accomplish with it. She is the most fascinating person I have ever known, and the complex layers of our lives are woven with the simple enjoyment of appreciating life on earth and being humble to the Creator and creation. However, not everyone can travel across the planet to find the love of his or her life like I did. For many, it must be recognized and accomplished by embracing a deeper worldview and using it to identify positive people in one's everyday environment. *The Love Ethic* can help with the development of this view.

Given the history of love on this planet, it is ridiculous we put a standard tag on love. It is completely unfair and limited. However, I think the notion of Black love in this book is an answer to the hatred that has taken place between Black men and Black women. Something has been poured in the waters of the Black community that has made hate and animosity more understood than love itself. Maybe it is time to turn that television, movie, or song off and search for love. Reading this book will hopefully respark the necessary conversation needed to find the love within ourselves to connect to one another again. Our history is based on love and looking out for one another. Today, our survival and growth amongst the chaos on the planet depends on us loving each other. Any community dialogue involving healing, relationships, or renewal will find this book an essential tool, thus making it possible to find and totally unlock the love that has been missing between the Black man and woman.

Peace.

Chuck D, Public Enemy

(THE) MOTIVATION

"All beauty is in the creative purposes of our relationships."

Ayi Kwei Armah

"The fall of a nation begins in individual homes."

Akan (African)
Proverb

First, we would like to start by thanking everyone who supported this work and our vision for Black relationships and families. This work has been a very long process. Like Black relationships themselves, it has been filled with much disagreement, introspection, and love, but it has finally come to fruition, and we are excited to share this process with you. This book is our gift to all Black people looking for happiness and fulfillment in their relationships. Some may ask why this book is important at this time and why we felt it had to be written. Now, we can give you the popular answer and say we were called to write it or the Creator ordained us to bring it forth. On some deeper level, that may be true, but in fact, this process has been a healing one for the both of us. Like many couples, we often struggle to love and respect one another in a world that makes it quite difficult to do so. Every challenge we successfully conquered together has made us stronger and more committed to our personal vision of creating the healthiest environment to love each other and nurture our children. Through this process, we have developed a larger vision for other Black people who may be seeking love, are happily in love, or are struggling to understand love. We also hope this book will inspire those who have chosen to give up on real love to continue their journey toward it.

We feel there are many reasons why brothers and sisters are having such a difficult time finding and loving one another. Some of these reasons have been outlined; others have yet to be identified, but we felt it was our duty as a Black couple to candidly discuss some of the issues we feel are obstacles to healthy Black relationships and hopefully offer solutions to finding and sustaining love.

We have heard many of our friends, both male and female, complain about one another repeatedly. Sisters were constantly complaining about brothers trying to be playas, womanizers, and ballers. If that wasn't bad enough, now many of the sisters we meet think they can't find a man because he is with a white woman or he is gay or "down low." One especially hurtful belief we observe comes from career-successful Black women who claim they need a man who is at least on their educational and financial level because they do not want to marry down.

One of our closest friends said, "I have spent all this time working on myself, and I at least deserve a man who is doing the same."

Sometimes, if a sister does find a man, he has to be able to buy her jewelry, cars, clothes, fancy dinners, and exotic vacations. If he is not able, then she sees him as not being a good provider. Many times, his woman berates him and tells him he is not being a good man.

Now our male friends are no better. Many think Black women are gold diggers and controlling or all sisters really want is a thug brother to handle them. Sisters are also seen as naggers or castrators. They are also portrayed as argumentative, aggressive, complainers, and unsupportive. Some brothers have called Black women "dream killers." They believe Black women are unsupportive and unwilling to help them work toward a common vision because they are too materialistic.

These are comments and feelings we have gotten from dozens of our friends, various members of our family, and numerous associates over the years. In no way is this meant to stereotype our brothers and sisters, but, if you were to take a personal survey among your friends and family, We am sure you may find similar answers.

We are not saying that people do not need to have standards. Standards are important in finding and choosing a good mate. Akilah often tells people that she and her girlfriend made lists of the traits they wanted in a man before she met Kamau. These lists had the regular items, including great lover, financially independent, educated, attractive, and so forth. However, she had other items that were important to her as well, such as a good sense of humor, spiritual, confident, sympathetic, understanding, and good listening skills. Akilah valued traits that talked about the character of an individual, along with his achievements. How will we be able to build strong Black communities when superficial ideas about what it takes to sustain relationships exist between the present and future mothers and fathers of our children? We hope this book educates, heals, enlightens, and emancipates many of our brothers and sisters from the hindrances that prevent them from developing self-affirming relationships.

The Love Ethic represents our belief that a beautiful love is waiting for everyone willing to do the work. Love, like many things, has values that must be upheld for it to take place. A large part of the work for Black people is realizing how oppression, misogyny, mistrust, lies, playa/pimp shit, gold digging, deception, inferiority, anger, and ignorance have been perpetuated within our community by a societal structure that is not conducive to (or interested in) nurturing real Black love. We want our brothers and sisters to go below the superficial surface and get to the love they deserve.

As Black people, we must understand we can do nothing without our relationships. We are a people of relationships. We always have been. Our families and communities are an interaction of complex and dynamic relationships. In fact, if we look back over our lives, we will probably find that many of the things we have been able to accomplish could not have been done without a relationship or two to help us along the way. So the next time you ask someone why the Black community is not moving, ask yourself:

- Where is my relationship to help it move?
- Where are my relationships at?
- Where am I at?

Hopefully, this book can help you find the answers to these questions.

At this point, you probably are wondering what makes this book any different from what I have already read about Black relationships and what is this vision they keep talking about?

To answer the first question, this book is very different from what you have seen before. What makes this book different is what makes it special and powerful. *The Love Ethic* presents a balanced perspective on relationships. It does not favor a male or female slant. Rather, it takes an honest look at Black relationships through a historical lens. Because, as a married couple, we have created a shared vision for our own relationship and have become committed to a broader vision of helping other Black people discover the love that is waiting for them, we understand the daily work required to maintain love between a Black man and Black woman. *The Love Ethic* gives well-researched information regarding Black relationships. It contains analysis that is meant to inform and educate the reader as to what is truly happening in the Black community and what the real problems and challenges facing Black families are. *The Love Ethic* is authentic. It was not written to capitalize on the pain of Black people or pretend like we have all the answers so we could give our expert opinion. It was written to help inform and heal Black families.

As for the second question, this book is definitely the fruit that has fallen from the tree of our own family vision. It is the physical manifestation of the principles that we attempt to live by, that is, the principle of togetherness. It is what some call "twinlineal."

The term "twinlineal" can be simply defined as male and feminine equality. There are no leaders. Rather, the couple forms a collective unit. We want twinlineal interaction, as opposed to matriarchy or patriarchy, because these terms are singular, do not reflect the cooperative nature of human relationships, and do not reflect the traditional structure of African American relationships. Furthermore, an inequitable relationship structure causes stress and strife within a relationship. Twinlineal interactions between couples prevent divisiveness from occurring.

Twinlineal is a principle that refers to balance. This balance is magnificently demonstrated when male and female energies work in loving partnership with one another. This balanced energy is very powerful, and it has the remarkable ability to create beneficial things once focused. We can clearly see this energy manifested in the creation of life, the ultimate creative endeavor. Often, our relationships are fertile, yet untapped, arenas in our lives. However, they have the potential to change our lives for the better. *The Love Ethic* will strive to help couples tap into the reservoir of potential energy that exists within their relationships. *The Love Ethic* is about couples finding their love power to create twinlineal relationships that lead to healthy, productive marriages.

There is a reason why we focus on marriage so intentionally. It is because marriage matters. Marriages are important to love. Marriages are the containers that house love. Marriage gives love its goals, direction, definition, and efficacy. Marriage is the ultimate institutional, cultural, and social expression of love. There is a reason why children in cohabitation contexts do not do as well as children in marriages. Marriage increases the level of commitment and dedication a few notches and changes the psychology of its participants. Like the educational system legitimizes learning and the medical establishment legitimizes healing, marriage legitimizes love and forms the foundation for the creation of the family.

"You're Making Me Feel Like I'm Weird"

We do not want for Black men and women who are not married or have no interest in marriage now to feel like one of our friends when we discuss the topic of Black relationships. She often says, "You're making me feel like I'm weird."

Let us be clear. The point of this book is not to make couples who do not last forever feel like failures. Some people are just not compatible. Nor is it to point the finger at single Black people and blame them for the problems in the community. This book will help those who are looking, might be looking, or will be looking one day to identify the value in marriage and Black love. This book is an attempt to convey the importance of marriage and love (and they are important) for the Black community and give our understanding of why things have somewhat broken down and what can be done to change things.

It is essential we understand the family is the cornerstone of the African American community. (It always has been, and it always will be.) Strong family units and healthy love relationships create happy and committed adults who then develop well-motivated and emotionally healthy children who are ready to compete within society. These type of relationships also help to generate wealth and property acquisition, which influences and benefits future generations. So we must begin to view our spouses and mates as partners and our families as foundations from which to build. This is why this book was so important for us to write at this time.

Many people told us not to waste our time writing a book on Black relationships. They said:

- "No one will buy it."
- "Black people don't read."
- "Black relationships are beyond repair."
- "Black love doesn't exist. Just lust."

But we do not feel this way. History has taught us that these views are incorrect. We have faith in Black people, and we have hope for the Black relationship. We hope, through this text, Black couples:

- Will reaffirm their dedication to one another
- Learn how to better communicate their dreams, challenges, and fears to one another
- Begin to view their relationships and family units as viable economic centers that build wealth for generations to come
- Create nurturing environments to raise productive and high-achieving children
- Create households that are full of love
- Begin to see their relationships as powerful tools to change the world
- Learn to trust each other again

We hope this book will help you understand why Black love is so beautifully difficult and that it will help you stop working out your individual pain, confusion, and stuff within the context of your relationship. But, most of all, we hope you find or rediscover your own peaceful, joyful, and powerful form of Black Love that will make all these hopes into realities. Our ancestors gave us a blueprint for relationships, *The Love Ethic*. We may have lost or forgotten it, but anything lost can be found again. Anything forgotten can be remembered. Possibly, this book can provide you with a window into your soul and some understanding regarding Black people's love story in America and give you permission to heal your own love hurts. Remember, "All beauty is in the creative purposes of our relationships." We get the most joy out of life when we are doing beautiful things with those we love most. Don't miss out on the blessings of relationships.

Peace, blessings, and love to you and your family from ours.

Kamau and Akilah

Passing down the Love Message

Mom, when I grow up, will I find a man who cares for me?
Girl, I don't know.
You just have to cross your fingers and see.

Mom, when I grow up,
will I find a man who will be my best friend?
Girl, you be lucky if you find a man who won't up
and leave you in the end.

Mom, when I grow up,
will I find a man who has a good heart?
Sweetie, that's hard because most men want to be apart.

Mom, will I find a man who works hard for his family?
Honey, many men out here are
choosing irresponsibility too easily.

Mom, has there been anyone you have loved and cared for?
That's a long story, but there was one man
who hurt me to my core.
He had a good heart, and he was very smart.
But the world just swallowed his pride and
chewed him up, and he lost his stride.

I tried to love him, but he became a shell of himself.
I didn't even recognize him.
It got so bad that our prospects
for being together became grim.
So, we decided to go our separate ways.
It still hurts me deeply to talk about it today.

See, I want you to find love,
but I don't want you to be disappointed.
This is a tough world for love,
and it feels like it never gets anointed.

Don't let my fears scare you from finding your soul mate.
As long as you work on yourself,
your love will surely be great.

Just believe that healthy and wonderful
Black Love is a possibility.
And, before you know it, you will be in the loving
place you vision to be.

John Richard Curtis and family (1921). This is the common African American family in the early twentieth century. Schomburg Center for Research in Black Culture, the New York Public Library.

The African American Experience: The Problem of Justice

"Love is what justice looks like in public."

Cornel West

LATE one night, we were both half-asleep in bed with the television on when we were suddenly jarred out of our peaceful slumber by Cornel West and these words, "Love is what justice looks like in public." The profoundness of this statement must have resonated with both of us because we each awakened and stared blankly at the TV for a minute without uttering a word. Finally, breaking the silence, Akilah said, "That has to be in the book." It was immediately agreed upon.

The concept of justice is an important one for any society and its citizens, but, until Dr. West's statement, we just associated it with lawyers, the criminal justice system, the courts, and the prison industrial complex. However, justice permeates every part of society. We often hear popular civil rights leaders say, "No justice, no peace." It demonstrates that African Americans will not rest until they feel they are receiving the love they deserve from society. Justice is how society and its leaders show love for their citizens. It's how the citizens know they are cared about. It makes living within the society meaningful, bearable, and logical. When people feel love from their society, they are more willing to sacrifice for it to run well because they know they will receive that love (justice) in return. People know others will not hurt them, steal from them, disrespect them, or abuse them without any consequences. These consequences occur because society loves them and wants to do right by them.

However, as African Americans, since the first African was brought to this country in shackles, we have never received justice or felt America's public love. Life in America has always been an uphill battle, a quest for justice. Whether it is in the social, economic, political, or cultural realm, Black people have seldom felt loved in this country. We have rarely known justice. At times, it feels like entire institutions and structures are against Blackness itself, denying us justice. It's common knowledge that financial institutions deny loans for Blacks more often than their white counterparts. Black men are more likely to be imprisoned than any other group of people in the United States. The American educational system, from grade school to higher education, has frequently failed African American students at several aspects of instruction. We could go on incessantly. One would be naïve to think the persistent lack of love that Black people receive in the American context does not take its toll on us. It does debilitate and demoralize us.

African Americans have never been members of this society, just citizens. It is important to understand the difference. Citizens are afforded the rights and privileges of law and politics. Societal norms and statues protect them. Employers cannot discriminate against someone because of race, gender, or age. The law in America protects these rights. However, members belong and are recognized as being part of the group. Members have a special right and are recognized as unique. They receive privilege, benefits, and love that are not afforded to nonmembers. Citizenship is lawfully driven; membership is socially driven. Blacks have rarely (if ever) been members of this nation. We have rarely received justice. Therefore, we have rarely received love. Have you ever heard of the police shooting fifty times at a white man?

No. It is because he is a member of white society and receives privileges. Have you heard of the police shooting fifty times at a Black man? Yes. He is a citizen, but not a member. He does not belong to the exclusive club and does not receive the special benefits. Being white in American society is like having a Black card (no pun intended); being Black is like possessing a credit card you are constantly trying to upgrade. What does this have to do with your love relationship? Ask yourself another question first. Can two people who consistently do not receive public love (justice) come together and love each other in a healthy and just way? Yes. However, it takes a hell of a lot of work! This book is our effort to assist that work.

Love is what justice looks like in public. If this is true, then Black people have never felt public love because we have never known collective justice. American political, cultural, economic, and social institutions have denied Black people justice for centuries. They have denied us love, and this process has caused us to deny ourselves love. We have been outsiders, much like a person standing on one side of a locked gate and gazing through. Being excluded and not truly accepted can bring up feelings of hopelessness and helplessness. For African Americans, these feelings live deep within and are activated repeatedly. Therefore, the first part of *The Love Ethic* we lost was the aspect of justice. We lost it the minute we stepped on these shores in shackles, and it has created everlasting love wounds. These love wounds, the wounds of oppression, must be healed.

Resulting from the lack of justice, Black people may begin to feel like everyone may be against us. No one can be trusted. This is extremely dangerous when we think about our love relationships. How can a person who is consistently shown little societal love be able to love deeply and freely? It often feels impossible. How do you go from surviving to thriving? How do you transition from coping to liberating? How do you move from adaptation to self-determination?

When we think about our ancestors and the hope and love they had to have in order for them to endure the circumstances of slavery, Jim Crow, poverty, and terror, we find strength in their strength. It is a magnificent testament to our human spirit in general and who we are as a people specifically that we continue to be a people of integrity and dignity who struggle for acceptance, love, and justice.

Nowhere has this constant struggle for justice more affected Black people than in our love relationships. Our relationships have been ripe with love, trouble, pain, and pleasure. There are reasons why our relationships look the way they do today. It pains us to hear Black people totally blame themselves for the current conditions of our love relationships. We want to help Black folks understand how things got the way they are. Things did not just happen. Circumstances were the by-product of many historical events. The question and the answer lie in our history. Therefore, it is necessary to go back and examine our peculiar love history in this country.

"Sankofa" is a West African term that, loosely translated, means "go back and fetch it." This is what we feel is necessary at this time. We need to look back in order to move forward. Rarely have we chosen to examine our past in America and contemplated the effect it has had on our love for one another. In the spirit of Sankofa, this book is an attempt to go back and fetch our love story.

The Love Ethic is essential for Black relationships to prosper. *The Love Ethic* states that there are essential values that are needed to have healthy and productive love relationships. How many of us have asked, "What is love?" Then we got nebulous answers that never really satisfy our need to know. We talk so much about this thing that we cannot define that it can become frustrating. If we do not know what it is, how do we know if we are doing it correctly? By going back into our history, we quickly learned the term "love" is comprised of a set of essential values. We felt this revelation was a revolutionary step in identifying when we feel love and when we don't. It is a monitor to tell if we are loving fully and when we are falling short. For many of us, we were never taught *the Love Ethic*, or we did not even know it existed. Love, like anything, must be taught and learned. Throughout time, various historical occurrences and institutions, such as slavery, segregation, poverty, and discrimination, have attacked the values making up *the Love Ethic*, causing Black men and women to lose touch with their Love Ethic and the values it contains that are necessary for healthy and productive relationships. We acknowledge that many of the problems facing Black relationships stem from various political, economic, and social forms of racism and discrimination. We in the Black community must deal with the realities of capitalism, racism, and sexism and the behaviors and consequences they create. However, to do this effectively, we must heal our relationships and reestablish our Love Ethic. We believe that many of our relationship problems are the result of a lost Love Ethic that has been forgotten due to the wounds inflicted by the various forms of oppression Blacks have had to endure in America. It is the memory of these past transgressions that are passed from generation to generation through stories and behavior within the community. We term this process as "Collective Love Wounds (CLWs). These CLWs do not just happen at the time of injury. They are passed on and permeate throughout a people's existence until a major disruptive event occurs. We all have these CLWs. One popular one that many Black women have is, "We can do bad by ourselves." Loosely translated, if a man is not bringing something substantial to the table (money), you do not need him. This may sound like common sense. Why would someone want anyone who cannot better her life? But it can be damaging when we think about the lack of justice (public love) that Black men have traditionally received in society. As you will read, Black folks get strength from being with each other, not from being apart. Separating Black men and Black women was a strategy that slave traders used because they understood it would weaken us if we saw ourselves as individuals. Only when we are united and loving each other are we a force to be reckoned with. Therefore, until our CLWs are dealt with, they always pose a threat to healthy relationship and community functioning. What makes matters worse is that we have never had the chance or luxury to rebuild this Love Ethic, rediscover our love for one another, or heal our love wounds, until now.

Chapter one describes the current reality of our love relationships. Chapters two to six take a look at pivotal historical eras and examine

the impact they had on *The Love Ethic* of Black people and how they
have contributed to our CLWs. In chapter seven, we attempt to make
sense of contemporary Black love. Chapters eight and nine examine
Black men and women, respectively, in an attempt to show the effect
the several historical eras have had on us as individuals trying to navigate love. The final chapter of the book outlines *The Love Ethic* and
seeks to provide tangible solutions to *The Love Ethic* dilemma within
the African American community.

This text is about healing, not just explaining. It attempts to start
a much-needed conversation within the Black community about love,
not infidelity, irresponsibility, or foolishness. It seeks to address the lack
of justice we have received as a people that has consistently attacked
our love of self and family.

We feel one final note about Black love must be said. In spite
of the horrific conditions, Black men and women have endured in
this country, we have still entered into loving relationships with one
another frequently. Throughout time, Black men and women have
seen the importance of these relationships as representing the only
semblance of normalcy we could achieve in our lives, so we valued
love, no matter how brief it was. Slaves were not allowed to get legally
married because that interfered with the slave master's economic
goals. However, our ancestors found ways to express their love for one
another. They used symbols, like jumping the broom, to express and
pledge their love and commitment to each other. Despite the horrible
conditions during Jim Crow, Black love carried on through sheer hope
and determination. Throughout urban decay, poor living conditions,
and disrespectful images forced upon us, Black love continued. Hope
was the thing that got our ancestors through their circumstances and
allowed them to persevere. They had a hope of finding peace, achieving
a better future for themselves and their children, surviving, and recap-
turing beautiful Black love. Hope became the focus of our people and
our relationships. Our forefathers and foremothers endured great pain
and frustration with the sole purpose being the belief that a brighter
day was around the corner for Black love. If they persevered under

their horrific circumstances and maintained their love for one another, we certainly can and must. This book is as much a celebration of their will and sacrifice as it is a depiction of Black pain and recovery. All beauty is in the creative purposes of our relationships. Our ancestors knew this. We must remember!

Do You Love Me?

I often ask myself, "Does America love me?"
We have a very violent past that began with slavery.
I convinced you I was more than three-fifths of a man.
As you saw during Reconstruction, many of us
had a successful plan.
After I demonstrated success, you took all my rights away,
had me working and living in abject poverty on
plantations with very little pay.
Then after you had no more use for me because of the
cotton gin,
I relocated my family and belongings up North to move in,
start a new life, and remind myself why
I love this country so.
But what I found was drugs, poor jobs,
and the urban ghetto.
I didn't let that stop me from loving you to your core.
I went to fight on your behalf and gave my
son to the Vietnam War.
When I got back from burying my son,
I knew for sure that my bad lot
with America was surely done.
I was wrong once again.
How could this be?
You killed off my leaders and then pulled the
resources outta my community.

There have been times when I thought
I might see some reciprocity,
but, when I looked closer, what I saw was
manipulation and hypocrisy.
So where do we go from here?
I'm not quite sure how to behave.
It seems like I'm always left to question my place in this
land of the free and home of the brave?

CHAPTER ONE

WHEN WORST COMES TO WORST, MY PEOPLE COME FIRST: THE PROBLEM OF ORDER

"The events which transpired 5,000 years ago, five years ago, or five minutes ago have determined what will happen five minutes from now, five years from now, or 5,000 years from now. All history is a current event."

Dr. John Henrik Clarke

While we lived in Atlanta, we made several friends. They were a diverse group of individuals who spanned from top executives at large corporations to day laborers and from the formally educated to the informally educated, but the conversations about relationship were similar, regardless of the economic standing. Our friends, regardless of whether they were married or single, pondered the problems of Black relationships and how they could be fixed. But, most importantly, who was to blame for why they look the way they do? The outcome of these conversations were usually Black men blaming Black women for being overbearing, controlling, and insensitive or Black women blaming Black men for being lazy, jobless, promiscuous, and incarcerated. This never got us anywhere. These conversations only developed more resentment toward one another. These conversations were partially the motivation for this project.

The blame game never solves anything. It usually just confuses the issue. But it does suggest that Black people know there are problems in our relationships that need fixing. At least that's a start, but a start is not an end point. We need to go deeper in our analysis and discussions regarding Black relationships and start asking, "Why?"

Standing up for Black love and Black relationships threatens several people. Many institutions and people make a lot of money and produce a lot of research off the private lives and social disorganization of Black life. We may ruffle some feathers by some of the strong stances we take in the book, but, in order for us to begin healing from our wounds and moving toward love, we need to be honest. We can't worry about how what we are saying is going to appeal to the public or who our affirmative stances will anger. Our love for Black life has to speak for itself. We love Black people, and we have dedicated our lives to the uplifting and healing of our community.

Let us get one thing straight. While single-parent households, which have been more common among Blacks in America in the post-Civil Rights era, have gotten us through tough times in this country, they are not optimal for Black men, women, or children. Those who suggest they are somehow left over from our times in Africa or natural to the African American experience are simply wrong. Anyone who does serious and informed study of traditional African civilization, philosophy, spiritual systems, or familial structure would understand that Africa is about balance, specifically male and female balance. It is not matriarchal or patriarchal; these two energies are balanced within the person and society. Africa was always twinlineal (balanced between male and female energy) in its composition. Don't be fooled by the way it looks today. Traditionally, Africans have always understood the importance of balance. Balance within family life was seen as especially essential.

The issues affecting Black relationships are unique and can differ greatly from those facing other groups. This difference stems from our distinct experience within American society and the oppressive historical relationship Black people have with America. Therefore, to examine Black relationships correctly, one must understand the role racism, oppression, and discrimination play in Black people's lives. Unfortunately, beyond recognizing the impact of American racism on Black individuals, few understand the deep and meaningful way it has affected Black relationships, both directly and indirectly. In this section, we hope to present an accurate account of the definitive issues that the African American community should be worried about from a relationship standpoint. By discovering the truth regarding our collective condition, we begin to truly see the real problems that prevent us from experiencing deep and committed relationships with one another. Truth brings about clarity of thought, helping us to experience higher realms of consciousness and possibilities. Only then can we begin solving the problems that plague our relationships and our families. Truthfully, Black relationships are in trouble in this country. Now this might not be news or shocking to most, but some of the following statistics and trends may be. All of which speak to the various amounts of disorder happening within the community presently.

- **During the days of slavery, a Black child was more likely to grow up living with both parents than he or she is today. (America for Divorce Reform, 2008)**

    When you consider the way the Black family was attacked during the institution of American slavery, it seems impossible to think that our families were more intact then than they are now, but they were. If this is not a severe warning signal, we do not know what is. When former slaves were interviewed, 82 percent reported the presence of their mothers during their early childhood years, whereas only 42 percent remembered having contact with their fathers. This is amazing when considering the instability that Black families had to exist in during slavery. Why are our modern families so unstable when we seem to have more control over them?

- **In 1920, 90 percent of Black families had both the mother and father present. This number dropped to 68 percent in 1970, 50 percent in 1990, and 30 percent in 2007. (BNET Research Center, 2000).**

This trend is extremely problematic because it shows how the two-parent Black family has declined over time. Why is this significant? All research we have ever seen on child outcomes suggest that children suffer greatly when two parents are not present and married to each other. However, it is also troubling because it suggests that two-parent households appeared to be very important to the Black community back in the day. Nowadays, it seems not so much, and our children may be suffering because of it.

- **Three or more years after divorce, the Black family's income remains 47 percent lower than if the parents had remained together.(America for Divorce Reform, 2008)**

- **It is estimated that, while the family income of white children rises by 45 percent when a single parent marries, the family income of Black children rises by 81 percent with marriage. (America for Divorce Reform, 2008)**

The great teacher/historian, Dr. John Henrik Clarke, used to say the family was the cornerstone of the nation. This is true economically as well. The above statistic clearly shows that part of the economic gap the Black community is suffering from in American society is tied up in our family's and our high divorce rate. In *Powernomics*, Claud Anderson calls for African Americans to spend and make money with one another. This becomes difficult to do with splintered families. Our money is not being focused and is being divided in too many ways. With the two-parent family unit, families are able to acquire more income and focus it. Two people working are better than one.

• **Today, the number of children born into a Black marriage averages less than 0.9 children per marriage. The birthrates of Black married women have fallen so sharply that, absent out-of-wedlock childbearing, the African American population would not only fail to reproduce itself, but would rapidly die off. (America for Divorce Reform, 2008)**

Married Black people are not having children. One of the main things marriage facilitates is the creation of children. Children are the future and hope of any people. Without them, there is no future of the people. But it seems our relationships are not producing them. Having children is apparently not the priority it once was.

• **In 2001, according to the United States Census, 43.3 percent of Black men and 41.9 percent of Black women in America had never been married, in contrast to 27.4 percent and 20.7 percent respectively for whites. (America for Divorce Reform, 2008)**

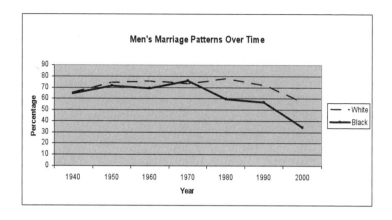

The decline in marriage among African Americans. National Center for Health Statistics, 1940–1990. U.S. Bureau of the Census, 2000.

- **African American women are the least likely in our society to marry. In the period between 1970 and 2001, the overall marriage rate in the United States declined by 17 percent. For Blacks, it fell by 34 percent..(America for Divorce Reform, 2008)**

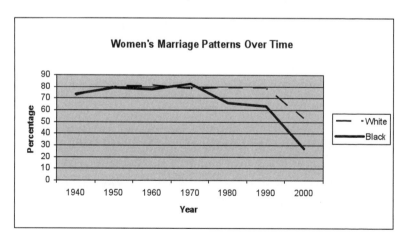

The decline in marriage among African Americans. National Center for Health Statistics, 1940-1990. U.S. Bureau of the Census, 2000

- By the age of thirty, 81 percent of white women and 77 percent of Hispanics and Asians will marry, but only 52 percent of Black women will marry by that age.(Institute for American Values, 2005)

What is stopping Black people from finding one another and creating the families we so desperately need as a community? We need to come together, and we need to do it earlier.

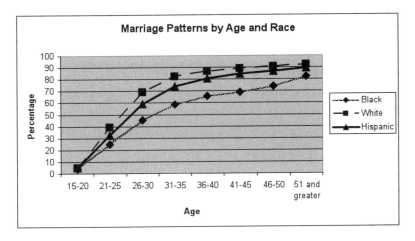

Original research conducted by Akilah Watkins-Butler using data from the University of Minnesota, the Integrated Public Use Microdata Series.

- **Nearly two million Black males are either currently in a state or federal prison or have been at one time. Experts add that almost 17 percent of Black men had prison experience in 2001, compared with 7.7 percent of Hispanic men and 2.6 percent of white men.(United States Department of Justice, 2000)**

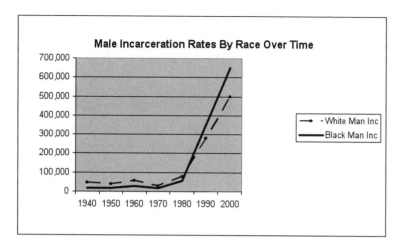

The Inter University Consortium for Political and Social Research, 1940–1980. U.S. Bureau of the Census, 2000

- **In 1980, one of every ten African American males was involved in the penal system. In 2007, one of every three African American males was involved in the penal system. It is projected that, in 2020, two of every three African American males will be involved in the penal system (Kunjufu, 2007).**

  The incarceration of Black men is the single-most destructive and important social problem facing the Black community in the twenty-first century, and it is profoundly impacting our relationships. It's making it nearly impossible to carry on healthy, productive relationships with one another. If we are to have relationships that work, we are going to have to reverse this trend.

- **More than eight hundred thousand African American males are in college. More than 1.6 million African**

American females are in college. African American
females graduate at a 10 percent higher rate than African
American males (Kunjufu, 2007).

The achievement gap between Black men and women
is another problem affecting the Black relationship.
What is happening with our Black boys within the
educational system that is causing them to lag behind?
We must understand that, as a society, we are not just
educating and raising Black boys. We are educating
and raising future fathers, husbands, and leaders
within our community. Our community and society
will pay tomorrow for the mistakes we make today.

- **Married men are less willing to engage in dangerous,
antisocial, or self-centered activities and more willing
to turn their activities toward the needs of a family..
(Institute for American Values, 2005)**

    Married men are less likely to participate in unhealthy
    behavior. Marriage matures men and changes their
    outlook on life and their responsibilities. They are
    more engaged in their wife and children's lives and less
    likely to fight, drink, and engage in criminal activity.

- **Married woman appear to have a lower risk of experiencing domestic violence than cohabiting or dating
woman..(Institute for American Values, 2005)**

    Women are less likely to marry violent men. Married
    people tend to invest in each other more than single
    people, so violence is less likely to occur. It is impor-
    tant to understand that domestic violence in the
    African American community is a significant issue

and should never be taken lightly. For young women thinking marriage is a good strategy for controlling a violent partner, it is not! However, statistically it does seem that married women do experience less violence.

- **Married men tend to make upwards of 40 percent more than single men with similar education and a job.** **.(Institute for American Values, 2005)**

  Married men tend to be more focused and strategic when it comes to their careers. They are more likely to eat right, get proper sleep, and go to the doctor more often. All of which are important to career success.

- **Marriage, not cohabitation, works best for individuals, children, and communities. .(Institute for American Values, 2005)**

  This may sound very controversial, but it is true. Marriage, not cohabitation, is what is optimal for individuals, children, and communities. Some may argue that it is love, not marriage that works best. However, when you look at the numbers, marriage matters. Women are less likely to be depressed, poor, and victims of domestic violence when married. Men are more likely to be employed, live longer, and have healthy emotional and mental health than their single counterparts. Children who are born to married individuals are more likely to have closer relationships with both their mothers and fathers, graduate from high school and attend college, and are less likely to engage in dangerous activities such as drugs and alcohol. Communities with higher rates of married couples are less likely to experience violent crime and have higher income residents, which help to fund much-needed services and schools. Cohabitation does not do this; marriage does. When individuals are married, they have made a commitment to themselves and the larger community. They have created a shared vision and made a commitment to work toward that vision.

Some of these statistics and trends are downright scary while others are unbelievable, but they are all true. We deal with many of them in this book. However, we want you to take two things from this chapter:

1. The problems facing the Black relationship and the Black community are huge and serious. We are at a crossroads in the development of the Black relationship and family. We must act to save our relationships, families, and communities. No one is going to heal our relationships for us. That is our work, and the current state of the Black community and family suggests this work must be made a priority. We are the ones who must take the responsibility to restore order. It is time we make our relationships and ourselves the focus of our attention. We must be a bit selfish and nearsighted. In the poignant words of the rap group Dilated Peoples, "When worse comes to worse, my people come first!" They come first in our minds, hearts, and scholarship. This book is the physical manifestation of these facts.

2. There is hope. Two Black people who love one another, have children, care about this issue, and are achieving things in their lives wrote this book. We found one another, and we are making it work. It isn't always easy, but nothing worth having ever is. When we recognize the source of strength and power that exists in our relationships with each other, we

will begin to lose the fears and worries that hinder our lives and happiness. Tremendous wealth and possibility can come from the love and wisdom that we share with one other. These opportunities are not available to some of us. They are available to all of us. We are linked together. So we must have faith in our relationships and the power and resiliency of Black people. We have made it through storms in this country before, and we will do it again, together!

Is It?

Oh Lord, who is to blame?
Who is to blame for the disorder of today?

Is it the gangs? Or is it the poverty?
Is it the policies? Or is it the economy?

Is it single mothers with no help?
Or is it absent fathers with no wealth?

Is it racism? Or is it sexism?
Maybe it's classism or just the system.
Is it the prisons? Or is it the drugs?

Is it cops? Or is it the thugs?
Maybe it's the suburbs or the cities.
Perhaps it's the impoverished or the too sidity.

Is it the TV, videos, or music?
Or it just might be the youth who consume it.
You know what?

It might just be the materialism of today or the trends,
which often say; you have to act or be a certain way.
Is it the community violence, which for some is all too real?

Perhaps it's the pain and inadequacy that some people feel.
Is it the scholars with their theories? Or the criminal justice
system with its juries.

Is it the teachers, schools, or students who are the true
shame?

Or is it the simple fact, that everyone is to blame!

Husbands, wives, and families sold indiscriminately to different purchasers are violently separated, probably never to see one another again (1853). Schomburg Center for Research in Black Culture, New York Public Library.

CHAPTER TWO

THE ENSLAVEMENT OF BLACK RELATIONSHIPS: THE PROBLEM OF TRUST

"Give my love to my father and mother and tell them good bye for me, and if we shall not meet in this world I hope to meet in heaven."

Abream Scriven,
a slave in 1858, in a letter he wrote to his wife
after being sold to another plantation.

As a child growing up in Brooklyn, New York, Kamau often had conversations about Black enslavement and history with family, friends, and elders, seeking answers to questions of Black history. However, the responses he too often received were:

- "That's in the past, and we must move on."
- "We invented the traffic light."
- "Why Black history? We are Americans."

Unfortunately, these explanations never seemed to be satisfying to him, so he started his own investigation into the history of African Americans. This led him to the work of John Henrik Clarke, Asa

Hilliard, Na'im Akbar, and Amos Wilson. These great thinkers all had various perspectives on Black history, but they all agreed that what we are taught in history class is not completely accurate history. It is distorted bits and pieces. So, it is no wonder Kamau received the kind of answers regarding Black history from so many brothers and sisters that he did. We seem to know little regarding Black history prior to 1617. In fact, you would think Black people appeared out of thin air as slaves. This is certainly not the truth, but, if we are unaware of our history, then it might as well be true. The institution of American enslavement is partially to blame for this unawareness. It has shaped African American reality in America since its inception. Its legacy has affected every aspect of African American life, and our relationships are no different. The institution of American enslavement of Black people has left an imprint on our relationships that must be explored.

The institution of American enslavement was a pivotal point in history for the African American relationship. This is a period where we feel the African American experience was one of trauma. In fact, scholars such as Joy Leary, author of *Post Traumatic Slave Syndrome*, have suggested this traumatic period has created negative values, behaviors, and thought patterns that have been passed down from generation to generation, ensuring social problems within the Black community and Black relationship. It's hard for us to imagine how our ancestors maintained healthy love relationships during this particular period of American history. The persistent trauma that Black people were under had to trickle down to the Black relationship.

In many ways, the reoccurring injury that was slavery is still with the Black relationship today. If not directly, it is at least in memory. Within this section, we would like to explore the trauma of African American enslavement and its effects on the Black relationship.

How We Loved in Traditional Africa

Why are we talking about Africa? We reference Africa because Black folks originally come from Africa. Therefore, we think it is important to understand how men and women related to each other before our enslavement. It gives us a glimpse into how our relationships looked before the entire trauma occurred. It reminds us that we have a rich love history that goes far beyond the problems of today.

We attended a couple's retreat where the facilitator asked us, "What did our relationships look like five hundred years ago (before enslavement)?" The question baffled us. We had no idea how to answer that question or what to say. We never thought of our love outside the realm of oppression. It led us to do some research about the social construction of African relationships before enslavement. Many would have us believe that ancient Africans conducted their relationships as polygamists with women being vastly oppressed by men. Nothing could be farthest from the truth. In *The Spirit of Intimacy*, Sobonfu Some describes love relationships as a song of spirit inviting two people to join together and share their spirits together. How many of us approach relationships with that level of maturity? Not many. Individuals could not become intimate unless spirit wanted them to. When Sobonfu Some talks about spirit, she is describing the omnipotent feeling that Black folks call God, a spirit greater than themselves. How many people wait for a spiritual message about a particular issue in their lives? Some of us listen to our inner spirit when we decide to play the lotto, buy a car, or decide to go for a new job. But how many of us listen to that inner voice or look for a spiritual message when we choose a mate?

In traditional African society, relationships were so much more than two individuals coming together. They were two families, communities, and lineages coming together and uniting. The community had to make a commitment to the couple to help provide the conditions that would nurture and sustain a loving relationship. And because relationships were reciprocal, the married couple had to make a commitment to spirit, themselves, and the community. This is essential to understand because many of us today believe we only live for ourselves, and this is simply not true. Our relationships affect many people and have far-reaching consequences for the health and vitality of our communities. The Institute for American Values found that communities with higher marriage rates among Black families had lower murder and robbery rates. This suggests that communities with high rates of committed relationships between men and women are healthier to live in.

The Institution of Black Enslavement

Probably the most misunderstood event in human history is African American enslavement. Most people do not quite comprehend the institution or its lasting effects on the African American community. The ramifications of slavery are numerous. It was not just about uncompensated work. It was more about lost cultural legacy. It is songs and tales we will never hear, people we will never know, events we will never acknowledge, and history we will never remember. It is part of ourselves that is forever lost. This is a major occurrence. Cultural and historical memory was disrupted, leaving us unsure about our place in history and the world. This has caused each successive Black generation great psychological pain and frustration as they attempt to fill in the lost memory a bit at a time.

The institution of Black enslavement began at the end of the fifteenth century (coinciding with the voyages of Christopher Columbus) and officially lasted until 1865. It was carried out throughout the world, depositing Black souls in the Caribbean, South America, Europe, and America. This process disrupted the natural rhythm of the African family and community. Many people are ignorant to the fact that Africans had tight and functioning family units and vast complex societies before they were kidnapped and brought to their various destinations. Slavery tore family units apart. It was a constant and consistent traumatic experience. Everyone reading this book has been a part of a family. Can you image waking up one morning believing your family to be intact, only to find your mother, father, and siblings being taken away and never to return? The following quotation from an enslaved African captures the pain of this process:

I myself had my wife on another plantation. The woman my master gave me had a husband on another plantation. Everything was mixed up. My other wife had two children for me, but the woman master gave me had no children. We were put in the same cabin, but both of us cried, me for my old wife and she for her old husband. As I could read and write I used to write out passes for myself, so I could go and see my old wife, and I wrote passes for the other men on the place, so they could go see their wives that lived off the place (Litwack, 1979).

More than an estimated 100 million Africans were taken from the continent and dispersed throughout the world. When you see Africa today, think about how its most precious resource was stolen, its people. Think about what effect that has had on the continent and you.

As stated earlier, slavery was more than just working for free. The dehumanizing practices that occurred daily to Africans were truly traumatic. Black men and women were seen as property and nothing else. White people controlled the state and enforced immoral rule over Blacks. For example, Black men were used as studs that could produce children, thus creating more income for their slave masters. Only the biggest and strongest Black men were bred. Men who were considered weak were castrated out of fear they would reproduce with female slaves and create weak offspring. A man's value was derived by his physicality, how sexually viral he was, and how many children he could produce.

White men strived to control Black women through their sexuality and reproduction by making her mate with particular slave men on the plantation that they viewed as physically viral. The goal was to develop the biggest and strongest slaves. Black women were seen as the most valued of the slaves because they could produce children. This served two purposes:

1. The slave master could consistently program Black children into being subservient through the mother, keeping the cycle of Black inferiority going.
2. The Black woman was an economic engine for white slave masters. She could constantly produce children that became his property. This became especially important in the late eighteenth century when it became illegal to transport slaves from Africa. Slave owners had to rely on the reproduction of their slaves to continue their enterprises.

Black women were vulnerable during slavery because they could be sexually violated at anytime by almost anyone. Slave masters constantly violated Black women, as did some Black men who wanted to mimic their slave owners. Rape was used as a tool to terrorize women and make them submissive. Women were routinely forced to have children with men who were not their husbands because childbirth was associated with economic gain. This was extremely dangerous and threatened the lives of many women, but it also helped to create the image of Black women as sexually loose, promiscuous, and irresponsible with their reproduction. We see this image today when we turn on television. We see this legacy played out when Black women are portrayed as sexual props in music videos or "baby mamas." In fact, the whole image of the welfare queen is a modern-day adaptation of how slave women were viewed, that is, loose women who were unable to be sexually or morally responsible.

How We Loved During Enslavement

Family cohesiveness was difficult for many Blacks during this time, but it occurred frequently. In spite of the horrific conditions, Black men and women entered into relationships with one another often. Black men and women saw the importance of these relationships as the only semblance of normalcy for their lives. Unfortunately, enslaved Africans were not allowed to get legally married because this conflicted with the slave master's economic goals. However, some slave masters allowed it because they knew slaves who were married with children were less likely to try to escape.

Slaves with children feared their children could suffer if caught, so they sacrificed their freedom to raise their children. However, many male slaves refused to get married because it meant never being free. Many slave men avoided marriage because it meant they would always be a slave or have to leave their wife and child behind if they ran. When asked if he had a wife and child, William Wells Brown replied:

> If I should have a wife, I should not be willing to leave her behind; and if I should attempt to bring her with me, the chances would be difficult for success (Osofsky, 1969).

Slaves were not allowed to practice traditional ritual weddings or even anoint their vows in their newly Christian religion. Slaves used symbols to illustrate their commitment to each other, such as jumping the broom, which represented marriage between Black men and women. Unfortunately, slave masters controlled who and for how long slaves could be married and how they reared their children. Many families during this time were matrifocal, headed by the mother, because the father and mother were not allowed to live with one another. This family system elevated the Black woman to a position of greater responsibility, influence, and power within the family than that enjoyed by Black men. These patterns were different than those in traditional West Africa where the family was the central unit and decisions were made between men and women, not by one or the other. Some have argued this is the basis for why Black men have tried to use their power over Black women because they feel their role in the family was minimized and the Black woman has been privileged over them. Black men and women were not allowed to truly fulfill their roles as husband and wife because of the constant instability, fear, and division that loomed over them.

The Problem of Trust

Before being brought to America, African men had strong and healthy identities, as did African women. They related to one another in relatively healthy ways. There was trust. But the trust we had for one another was severely damaged during enslavement. This had serious ramifications for our relationships today.

We remember when we visited the slave castles in Accra, Ghana, and viewed how they separated the male and female slaves. They separated the men and women from each other and contained them in unsanitary and inhuman conditions. The reason for this separation was to weaken the power of the enslaved Africans. If enslaved African men and women were put together, they would have drawn strength and inspiration from one another and perhaps overtaken their captures. However, because they were separated, their power was diluted, and their spirit was weakened. Black men and women used to seek strength from each other. Unfortunately today, too many of us feel the opposite. We feel that being in a relationship steals our strength and power. How many times have we said, "I could do better by myself" or "I am carrying you"? Have we have lost the ability to depend on one another?

In addition to the separation during the Middle Passage, the plantation further disrupted the trust between Black men and women. The forcing of Black women to have sex with white slave owners created an early rift between Black men and women. The rift stems from the inability of Black men to protect Black women from this degradation and humiliation that accompanied this situation. Because white men were sexually violating their wives and mates, the humiliation that Black men felt was too much for some to take. The following passage from Sam Watkins, a Tennessee slave, shows the frustration of the Black male with this heinous condition:

He would ship their husbands [slaves] out of bed and get in with their wives. One man said he stood it as long as he could and one morning he just stood outside and when he got with his wife he just choked him to death. He said he knew it was death, but it was death anyhow, so he just killed him. They hanged him (Rawick, 1972).

This passage shows what the Black male had to endure during this time and how he had to swallow his masculinity on a daily basis. The situation was comparable to death. In fact, it was death of his manhood.

For the Black woman, this condition created a sense of resentment and fear. It promoted the notions that:

- The Black woman could not depend on the Black man for safety
- The Black woman had to depend on herself

Only the Black woman's strength and resolve could help her to survive. This was the initial psychological separation between Black men and women, and it was a major reason for the disruption of trust between Black men and woman.

The Black man lost trust in the Black woman because the Black woman was in ever-present danger and he could not protect her from violation, so his manhood was called into question and attacked constantly because of this situation. He could not depend on the Black woman to validate his sense of masculinity. Therefore, he could not trust her or his masculinity around her. Similarly, the Black woman lost trust in the Black man because he could not protect her from exploitation and violation, and she resented this.

Psychologically, when you cannot protect the ones you say you love, it becomes very difficult for trust to be fostered. Trust within a relationship is a feeling that comes from stability and knowing you are safe with the person who you love. This was impossible during slavery. A former slave illustrated the unsafe and unstable environment of American enslavement as he discussed his experiences on a very large cotton plantation. He described the differences in the way he and his wife were treated:

> My wife fared better than I did, as did the wives of some of the other Negroes, because the white men about the camp used these unfortunate creatures as their mistresses. When I was first put in the stockade my wife was still kept for a white in the 'Big House' ... When I left the camp my wife had had two children by some of the white bosses, and she was living in a fairly good shape in a little house off to herself ... Of the first six women brought to the camp, two of them gave birth to children after they had been there more than twelve months—and the babies had white men for their fathers (Meltzer 1983).

The unstable conditions and terror that enslaved Blacks lived with, coupled with the humiliation and fear they had to endure, fostered the loss of trust between Black men and women. This loss of trust is alive and well today within our relationships.

Slavery robbed us of our innocence and ability to Truly Rely Upon our Social Ties (TRUST) with one another. We see this every time we say a Black business is inadequate or when we say "Black people are not good workers. We see it when we do not look out for one another when we have an opportunity to do so. Our healing has to begin with trusting ourselves and finding our love for each other again. Only when we trust can we drop the negative memories that slavery tried to indelibly mark in our minds and hearts. With trust, something immense opens up. Hardship and strife no longer defines life. It becomes full of the potential and possibilities that a union between a Black man and Black woman can produce. When our heart becomes innocent and we trust ourselves and others, our scars disappear. We are filled with love and hope. Nothing and no one can ever take that feeling of love and hope away from us again.

Letter to the Ancestors

Dear those known and unknown,

Thank you for creating civilization, philosophy, and writing. Your great feats enable me to teach my son that he is capable of great academic and intellectual excellence when others tell him he isn't. Also, I appreciate the way in which you sacrificed and suffered, all the while with your eyes on a better tomorrow for me. Your strength is an inspiration I use every day. I tap into your ancestral memory every time I conceive a magnificent thought or idea. I use your historical guidance every time I am faced with seemingly insurmountable circumstances. And, yes, I look into your essence and feel your presence every time I hold my son.

Therefore, every day, I attempt to repay your gifts by being the best man, husband, and father I can be.

That is how I say thank you for all you have done for me!

Sincerely,

Kamau

Lynching of C.J. Miller, at Bardwell, Kentucky, July 7th, 1893. Schomburg Center for Research in Black Culture, The New York Public Library.

CHAPTER THREE

THE NADIR OF BLACK LOVE: THE PROBLEM OF HARMONY

Southern trees bear a strange fruit.
Blood on the leaves and blood at the root.
Black bodies swinging in the Southern breeze.
Strange fruit hanging from the poplar trees.

Billie Holiday and Lewis Allan
"Strange Fruit"

After it had been hanged and cut down by one mob and before it
had been burned in a city hall bonfire by a second mob, the body
of William Turner, Negro, aged 19, was hauled through Helena
to provide a moving target for white men armed with pistols who
lined the principle streets of this town and took pot-shots at it.
Turner had been hanged earlier for allegedly assaulting a white
telephone operator. Turner's corpse was roped to the rear of an
automobile and driven up and down the main streets of Helena
at various speeds as white men hooted, yelled, and perfected their
marksmanship by shooting at the almost-disintegrated remains.
No colored folks were allowed on the streets. When the celebrants
had had their fill, the body was burned. August Turner, father

of the mob victim, was summoned to the park to remove his son's charred remains.

Helena ARK,
November 18, 1921 (Ginzburg, 1996)

The preceding passage is one excerpt from *100 Years of Lynching*. It depicts the type of horrors Blacks had to endure during the "Nadir period," the name used by scholars to describe the time following Reconstruction that usually begins around 1890 and ends right around 1920. (Some argue it lasted as long as 1940.) The term "Nadir" suggests that times were as bad as or worse during this period than at any other time for Blacks. Yes, it was even worse than slavery

As it related to our intimate relationships and families, Black men and women were trying to pull their families back together during this time. Many were torn apart during slavery. We all have the mental picture of families being sold to different owners and children being torn from their parents. The Nadir period is the story that takes place after slavery ended. It is the era that we visualize Blacks searching the dangerous Southern countryside, looking for their loved ones and attempting to piece back their relationships and families. This clearly demonstrates the deep love we had for each other. We knew we needed each other. We relied on and needed the love of our family. This action demonstrated quite a bit of courage, dedication, and faith. Many former slaves were faced with potential death if they were caught in the wrong place at the wrong time, but they persevered through their fear in an effort to piece back their families and find their loved ones.

Blacks could not just focus on rebuilding their relationships and families; they also had to develop ways of taking care of themselves financially. The federal and state laws at the time made it nearly impossible for Blacks to make a living. After enslavement, whites still needed Blacks. We weren't totally worthless in their eyes. We were a valuable and exploitable commodity used to create profit by picking cotton and working the land. However, during this time, African

Americans began to rebuild their families, seek opportunity, and accomplish goals. During this physically dangerous and economically oppressive time, many Blacks held political office, created vibrant communities, and became educated. Many of the historical Black colleges and universities were also created. More than three thousand public schools were created in the South, laying the groundwork of public education for African Americans. From 1870 to 1877, there were six hundred and thirty-three state legislators, two state senators, and fifteen congressional representatives who were Black. Historically, Blacks are extremely politically active, and they have moved to be self-reliant and take control of their communities. So the next time people tell you that Black folks can't organize anything or build institutions and movements without assistance, remind them of this very powerful time in American history. Also, if African Americans organized themselves in such a focused and strategic way on the heels of slavery, imagine what we can do today with all our financial ability and education.

However, racist legislation quickly stopped the upward mobility of Blacks. Blacks were deemed unfit to run for office, and their rights were systematically taken away. Unfortunately, Black empowerment threatened many whites' feelings of superiority, so violence against Blacks ensued. Groups like the KKK began to form. Movies like *The Birth of a Nation* were created to stoke the fires of hate. (Incidentally, if you have not seen this film, you should. It will make many things about American racism much clearer. President Woodrow Wilson actually showed this flick at the White House.) The movie depicted Black men as uncontrollable and in need of white supervision. It tapped into white men's fear at the time that freed Black men would sexually assault white women. So Black men's sexuality had to be policed and harnessed. During slavery, Black men's sexuality was controlled and used to produce children that brought profit to the slave master. During the Nadir period, the Black man's sexuality threatened many whites so it had to be constantly controlled. This is why we read so much about castrating Black men during this time.

Once Black men were castrated, they were not in a position to fulfill many of the requirements of manhood. Whites used force and intimidation incessantly during this period. Remember, under the system of slavery, whites still supervised Blacks. During Reconstruction, Blacks were becoming independent and distanced themselves from whites somewhat. This distance made some whites uncomfortable, and it often caused a significant backlash. Consider the Rosewood Massacre that happened in Levy County in central Florida. In 1923, a white mob slaughtered over three hundred Black people over a Black man allegedly assaulting a white woman. (In *Rosewood*, John Singleton did a great job showing how blacks were successfully rebuilding their lives after slavery and Reconstruction to create industry, opportunity, and political power and how this threatened some whites.) This is a common narrative in the Black American historical record.

During the Nadir, Blacks were terrorized for their apparent threat to the white American way of life. "While the ending of slavery led to reconstruction of national politics and economics, it was not a radical reconstruction, but a safe one" (Zinn, 2005). As a result, Blacks became public enemy number one and lived in constant fear for their lives during the Nadir period, even more so than while enslaved.

The Nadir of American Race Relations

During the Nadir period, violence was used to keep Blacks in their place and noncompetitive within the market place. The Nadir period was made possible because of Reconstruction's failure. Both the North and the South played a role. "During this time, white Americans, North and South, joined hands to restrict Black civil and economic rights" (Loewen, 2005). Many white Americans at the time believed whites were superior and Blacks were inferior. Blacks were considered biologically inferior. Many scientists at the time claimed the Black brain was different than the white brain, and that meant it was deficient. Many postulated that Blacks were direct decedents of primates and were socially retarded, not having the intellectual capacity to read or understand complex systems and procedures. Black people were seen as children, hence the name "boy" or "girl," popular nicknames used to refer to Blacks of this time. These beliefs laid the foundation for Jim Crow, Northern segregation, lynching, and other forms of physical and psychic violence against Blacks.

In addition to physical violence like beatings, hangings, castrations, and murder, segregation ran rampant. The extent and intensity of this type of oppression is illustrated in the following passage:

> Jackie Robinson was not the first Black player in major league baseball. Blacks had played in the major leagues in the nineteenth century, but by 1899 whites had forced them out. In 1911 the Kentucky Derby eliminated Black jockeys after they won fifteen of the first twenty-eight derbies. Particularly in the south, whites attacked the richest and most successful African Americans, just as they had the most acculturated Native Americans, so upward mobility offered no way out for Blacks but only made them a target. In the North as well as the South, whites forced African Americans from skilled occupations and even unskilled jobs such as postal carriers (Loewen, 2008).

This passage clearly illustrates how Blacks fully participated in American society before the Nadir period was imposed. This period in American society was open season on Black people in America. This period was by far the most overtly racist time in American history:

> It is almost unimaginable how racist the United States became during the Nadir. From Myakka City, Florida, to Medford, Oregon, whites attacked their Black neighbors, driving them out and leaving the towns all white. Communities with no Black populations passed ordinances or resolved informally to threaten African American newcomers with death if they remained overnight (Loewen 166).

It is imperative that people understand the Nadir period was a national phenomenon, not just a Southern thing. It was an American thing. African Americans had most of their rights revoked during this time, and government intervention was nonexistent. The atrocities were numerous and very detrimental. Some of the major atrocities during (and leading up to) the Nadir period are in the following chart:

Nadir Occurrence	Consequence for Blacks
Compromise of 1877	The white citizens of the North turned their backs on the Blacks in the South. Southern whites gradually started to violate the rights of southern Blacks.
Plessy vs. Ferguson (1896)	This Supreme Court decision upheld segregation.
Blacks forced out of Major League Baseball (1889)	This action segregated Major League Baseball until Jackie Robinson broke the color line.
Kentucky Derby bans Blacks (1911)	This action helped segregate horse-racing jockeys for decades.
Mississippi Plan (1890)	In defiance of the fourteenth and fifteenth amendments, Mississippi legally took away Black's citizenship in that state. In 1907, Oklahoma followed suit.
The Bronx Zoo exhibits African male behind bars (1907)	This exhibit suggested that Blacks were seen as animals.
Minstrel shows (1880s and 1890s)	These works portrayed African Americans as bumbling, moronic fools, demeaning Black humanity.

Presidential election (1892)	Grover Cleveland won the election off the strength of racist rhetoric and the promise to deny rights to Blacks.
The Birth of a Nation (1915)	This is maybe the most racist movie ever made. It played a major role in the rise of the Klu Klux Klan in America and helped shape the notion of Black men as something to fear and white women as something to protect.
Tulsa riot (1921)	Whites dropped bombs of dynamite on a Black ghetto, destroying over eleven hundred homes and killing more than seventy-five people.
Riot of Springfield, Illinois (1908)	White mobs drove out two-thirds of the Black population, making it predominately an all-white town for generations.

Compiled from *My Teacher Told Me: Everything Your American History Textbook Got Wrong* (Loweman, 2008)

Imagine if all your rights were no longer legally significant and your humanity was openly challenged. The fear and apprehension you would feel would probably be paralyzing. How would you deal with it?

How the Nadir Period Affected Black Relationships

It is extremely important to discuss this time in history because of the terror that Black folks experienced and how it affected our ability to love. Also, it is important to paint a picture of the environment that love had to exist in during this time. We all know it is difficult to love your partner when the rent or mortgage is late or if one or both of you are unemployed. Imagine trying to love each other under the constant threat of fear and death. How stressful would this be? How successful would your efforts to love be? During the Nadir period, our peace of mind was robbed. This was a time of many lynchings of Black men, women, and children. We did not feel safe, and our ability to protect our families and ourselves was constantly tested. How could you love and be fearful at the same time? Fear robs us of our ability to love deeply because we cannot fully be who we are.

But one of the unintended consequences of this time was Black people's reliance upon one another to grow and survive. Black men and women had to depend on one another and create extended families. In 1920, 91 percent of African American children were born to a two-family household (Kunjufu, 1993). We married more than any other people in the United States. Today, that figure is at 30 percent. From 1880 to 1910, about 56.3 percent of Blacks had a mother and father in the home, and about 23.5 percent were extended family households with cousins, grandparents, aunts, and uncles in the household. Only 20.3 percent of families were fragmented or broken homes, meaning either a single mother or single father led them (Mandara and Murray, 2005). This is very different from where we are today. By the mid-twentieth century, family structure changed. Between 1950 and 1996, the percentage of Black families headed by married couples declined from 78 percent to 34 percent (Mandara and Murry, 2000).

What is happening to our sense of reliance upon one another now that was not happening during this dangerous period in American history?

The Problem of Harmony

Webster's dictionary defines "harmony" as "a pleasing or congruent arrangement of parts." Harmony is central to the formation of a successful union. The Nadir period disrupted that harmony from the outside in. Relationships have what we like to call "rhythm," a natural way in which they progress. It is a harmonious way of developing. Unfortunately, social structures and societal norms often have a way of disrupting that rhythm.

Harmony is the organizing principle of any relationship, especially a love relationship. It makes successful living arrangements possible. "Human beings cannot function in chaos, and out of the chaos of life they create an ordered [harmonious] existence" (Ani, 1994). Harmony is different from peace in that it does not imply that there is no conflict. It simply states the relationship is ordered in a certain way that always allows for positive development even when there is disagreement. Without harmony, arguments become fights, and obstacles become problems that lead to the disintegration of the family.

Harmony also implies work. It is hard but worthwhile work to strive to come to a congruent arrangement that works for all parties involved. Without harmony, work stops because people begin to ask, "What's the point?" Harmony is dedication personified. It takes dedication to align a relationship in a harmonious manner. This is not a sweet-pie-in-the-sky concept. It is a real and pragmatic thing to work toward harmony. Harmony is not an easy thing to bring about. It takes sacrifice and commitment on the part of the individuals involved in the relationship, but it also requires a supportive environment. It is something Black couples during the Nadir period did not have the luxury of.

The nadir period presented great problems for harmonious relations between Black men and women. Roles and responsibilities could not be cemented in the family. For example, men were not able to fulfill the roles as family protector and provider because America viewed him as less than human. How was he going to work to feed his family when so many legal and social restrictions were placed upon him?

Black women also struggled with their status in American society. They were seen as the workhorses for their families, husbands, and communalities. They still hold this status today. When did they ever have a chance to be at peace? Never. Black women's femininity has always been used against them in this country as countless forces vie for control of it.

During the Nadir period, many African Americans lost hope; family instability and crime increased. This period of American life, not slavery, marked the beginning of what some social scientists have called the 'tangle of pathology' in African American society (Loewen, 2005).

Now, we do not believe this era was the beginning of a tangle of pathology, but it certainly did its part to hurt Black relationships by attacking the harmony that existed within the community.

Many believe harmony's greatest threat is chaos, but that perspective is inaccurate. Harmony is born out of chaos. In a strange way, harmony needs chaos at some point to come into being. This is called the "unity of opposites." Harmony and chaos are not opposed; they are two sides of the same coin.

Harmony's greatest threat is fear, not chaos. Fear creates the climate necessary within the community and individual for harmony to be impossible. It causes an individual to default to caring about himself or herself and his or her personal well-being. In a time of fear, working toward interaction that is harmonious is quite difficult. Some of the consequences of fear and how they impeded harmony within Black relationships during the Nadir period are listed:

1. **Trust.** The Nadir period further attacked the trust that was eroded during enslavement. The fact that Blacks had to live constantly in fear of violence and mistreatment severely disrupted harmony within Black relationships. Black women could not trust Black men to protect them from societal exploitation and maltreatment; Black men could not trust anyone to protect them from angry white mobs and degradation. This fostered distrust among Black men and women on a subconscious level.

2. **Dread.** The Nadir period threatened Blacks in general and Black men specifically with a horrible and humiliating death. The threat of something that can kill you in a dreadful way causes much more fear than the thought of dying of heart disease. This dread creates passivity and apprehension and does not allow for the courage needed to create harmonious environments.

3. **Control.** The Nadir period and the fear it developed in African Americans nurtured the need for control. When one is confronted with perpetual fear, a need to control his or her environment and those in it is fostered. This would explain the development of control issues within African American relationships. Harmonious relationships cannot exist where control issues are rampant.

4. **Uncertainty.** The more uncertain a person is, the more likely he or she is to protect himself or herself physically and emotionally. This may cause one to guard his or her emotions and become avoidant of intimacy. People may say, "Doesn't stress and strife bond people together?" In the short term, it does, but, over the long term, it does more to disturb harmony than assist it.

5. **Awareness.** As the climate of fear worsens, our awareness of the situation increases. We become hyper-vigilant or quick to defend ourselves. We are sensitive to every wrong done to us. So little things done by loved ones become major issues and hurts. We lash out at anyone we interpret as threatening us, whether that is his or her intention or not. We sometimes see this with school-children who come from impoverished or violent communities. At school, when a teacher confronts or challenges them, they lash out because they are so used to defending themselves. This is similar to the climate created by the Nadir period. It does not nurture harmony among relationships.

If you are experiencing any of these issues in your relationship today, we ask you to reflect upon the origins of these issues. They may have deeper roots than you know.

Worse than the lynching, burnings, riots, and persecution, fear was the worst thing to come out of the Nadir period. It stole much from us as a people. It affected and changed Black relationships forever and left a legacy we are still dealing with today. Fear is crippling. It is like a cancer that eats away at everything vital that is needed to live.

Akilah has a T-shirt that reads, "Fear Kills." Every time she wears it, people stop her and say, "That's right, girl" or "No doubt." When people see the shirt, they get it! They understand that fear kills your hopes and dreams. Fear kills your ambition. Fear kills your faith. During the Nadir period, fear killed our harmony, and we have struggled to get it back.

We need to exercise our collective sense of courage, just like those brave souls who ventured into the dangerous Southern countryside while looking to reconnect with their loved ones. We need courage today, that is, the courage to love ourselves and love each other. Our history cannot be a burden to us. Rather, it has to be a sense of strength that we use to love each other more deeply. Only then will we begin to see our fear fall away and our harmony take center stage. Through loving each other, we can begin to put our world and relationships back together again, harmoniously.

A Thought Before Leaving

I know they coming to kill me, and my heart is full of
visions of death and fear.
Not knowing my fate is better than my children and
wife not being here.

He disrespected my wife and child.
Can you believe in front of me?
Hell no! If I allowed him to do what he wanted,
what type of man would I be?

Maybe I should get my gun and fight, like so
many brothers before me?
But that will just bring a bigger mob who will reveal
in its destructive glory!

No, I have to leave my family so they will be all right.
I can't even tell them where I be. I must leave tonight.

For they safety and they well-being,
I can't be with my family right now, so I better be leaving.

I hope they know my absence breaks my heart
because I don't want to go or be apart.

Oh Lord, my death might be fearful, but it may
be better than this cursed life.
God take care of my home, my children, and my
dear and beautiful wife.

Negro family living in crowded quarters, Chicago, Illinois, April 1941.
Schomburg Center for Research in Black Culture, New York Public
Library.

CHAPTER FOUR

THE PROMISED LAND, A DREAM DEFERRED: THE PROBLEM OF RECIPROCITY

"Uless began to wonder whether the clerk was going to sell him a ticket at all. Finally, she said, in a simpering, disgusted tone, 'Chicago, Chicago,' as if to show Uless that he might be able to take a bus to the North, but in her opinion, he was just another nigger."

Nicholas Lemann
Promised Land

Black must embrace Black
From the ghettos to the hills,
from the working class to the prison class,
from the children to the communities,
from the haves to the have-nots,
Black must embrace Black
and realize that Black can never separate
itself from Black.
"Black Must Be Beautiful Again,"

Marina the Poet

One of life's beautiful things this project has taught us is whenever things appear to be at their most difficult, the Creator always sends a solution in the form of a person, activity, or situation. This proved to be a very difficult chapter for us to write, so the Creator sent us Mr. Timuel Black, an educator and historian who has lived in Chicago for decades. He is ninety years old, and he has seen and done much. This gentleman was alive during Pearl Harbor and remembers how it changed the country. He taught the now infamous Jeff Fort when Jeff was just a child growing up on the South Side of Chicago. He remembers the great migrations of Blacks northward vividly. He truly has a wealth of knowledge and information. Mr. Black is certainly a Jegna (master teacher) in the West African tradition. He came to SSA, the school of Social Service Administration at the University of Chicago, where Kamau attends, to give a talk to students and unknowingly assist us with the shaping of this chapter. Much of this chapter is attributed to what we learned that day from Mr. Black. In the words of Dr. Charles Payne, one of Kamau's professors, listening to elders like Mr. Black is "how you learn history." Mr. Black truly helped us to understand the phenomenon of the Black migrations north, Black people's quest for the promised land, and the formation of the Black urban ghetto in America.

The First Great Black Migration

Black people have been migrating north from the South for generations. We all have that uncle and aunt we went Down South to stay with during the summer. For Kamau, it was his Uncle Junior in Georgia. For Akilah, it was her entire family on her mother's side in North Carolina. Northern Blacks have deep Southern roots that stem from years of migration northward. The first great migration took place around the early twentieth century as newly educated Blacks attempted to flee the tyranny of the Nadir period in the South. These migrants were looking for opportunity that did not exist in the South. Many of these Blacks were educated at our famous historically Black colleges and universities. They could not do much with their degrees in the South so they moved to the North. They moved for jobs that were situated in the North that required cheap labor. Because our ancestors were educated and would work for cheap, they fit the bill. But our ancestors did not just move for jobs. They moved for survival, the main goal of any group. In order to survive, you must be able to control your environment—socially, politically, and economically. Our ancestors moved north for the right to vote and so their children could obtain an education and escape tyranny. They also moved for hope, which is essential to living. Blacks of the time had hopes and dreams that were not being fulfilled in the South. The North served as an opportunity to realize those dreams. Many Blacks moved northward to what they thought would be a new start ripe with promise and possibility.

The first Black migration northward in the early twentieth century consisted of sophisticated men and women. They had what some would call a "middle-class mentality." They had an agenda for their move northward. That agenda was to attempt to gain greater control over their environment. That is exactly what they did. Blacks of this first migration created tight-knit communities where doctors lived next to number runners. A sense of sharing permeated the entire neighborhood. There was a belief we were in this northern experiment together. This belief in sharing and community was the physical manifestation of the principle of reciprocity.

The Significance of Reciprocity

Reciprocity is a very important concept for any relationship, family, or community. It is the ultimate manifestation of the African belief that "a person is a person through other persons." That is, communities, families, and relationships care for one another and provide mutual support for one another. It is more than just treating each other well. It conveys a connection and need between people, being a person in this world only means something in relationship to my brother or sister. I am because we are. This has always been the deep connection that Black people throughout the Diaspora share. Reciprocity demands a like response, meaning that good acts inspire more good acts. Caring behavior initiates more caring activities within a community or relationship. Reciprocity, when done correctly, is about love. It is love conveyed one act at a time that flows from person to person, improving the lives of not only those involved in the reciprocal act, but the lives of others around them.

Reciprocity is also about accountability. If you get back what you put out, then it behooves you to put out good acts and thoughts and take responsibility for negative behavior because it is coming back to you. The principle of reciprocity helps maintain functional and healthy relationships by connecting your individual well-being to the well-being of your mate, family, and community. Any relationship that is not reciprocal is a dead relationship. When we practice reciprocity, we ensure people always get back what they deserve and are never victimized because we are connected to them. To abuse others is to abuse ourselves. To deceive others is to deceive ourselves. To betray others is to betray ourselves. Reciprocity ensures we always treat one another with the respect and dignity we deserve. It suggests that, if we love ourselves, we will love others as well. Reciprocity demands we rely on each other because we are connected and need each other to be happy.

Reciprocity is about understanding we are in this life together as a couple, family, and community. This was the way of life for the first Black migrants to the North all those generations ago. They understood the importance of reciprocity.

The Second Great Migration

The second great Black migration in American history occurred between 1930 and 1970. During this period, five million African Americans left the rural South for the promised land of the urban North. This remarkable phenomenon is known simply as the "Great

Black Migration." It changed Black life in America forever (Lemann, 1992). This second migration was a very different group of people than the first because their motivations for moving were somewhat different from the first wave. This second group came to the North because they had little choice. With the invention of the cotton picker, sharecropping was virtually made obsolete. The cotton picker could do the job of one hundred sharecroppers; so many Southern Blacks were suddenly out of work. This historical event forced many more Southern Blacks north to look for work. However, this second wave was not as educated or sophisticated as the first wave. This second migration consisted of individuals who had experienced years of educational and economic neglect in the South. They were not as prepared to come north as the first migration.

Simultaneously, while this new group was being driven northward, a new law was being passed that restricted housing discrimination. The Fair Housing Act of 1968 made it illegal to "discriminate in the sale, rental, and financing of dwellings and in other housing-related transactions based on race, color, national origin, religion, sex, familial status." On the surface, this was a great accomplishment for the Civil Rights movement, but one of the unintended consequences was the creation of the Black ghetto and the loss of reciprocity.

The Problem of Reciprocity and the Black Urban Ghetto

The harsh realities that Blacks faced when they moved north are a well-documented fact. Many know about the riots, beatings, and discrimination. It is a matter of historical fact that whites have traditionally not wanted to live next to Blacks. However, what isn't as well known is the way progress has affected the living arrangements among Blacks themselves and how these occurrences have affected our communities and our love.

The Fair Housing Act allowed Blacks access to venues and housing options they did not previously have. Many who took advantage of this newfound possibility were either directly from the first migration of Blacks northward or from their lineage. However, this event left the new migrants coming from the South without the assistance or experience of the previous migration. New opportunities made it easy for the first migration to flee its obligation to the new migrants. The reciprocity that had long benefited the Black community was eroding from the inside out.

These conditions left an uneducated and unskilled second migration to fend for itself in a new hostile environment. The following assisted the decline of the second migration:

- Public housing (erected to contain this population)
- Tracking of Black students in public education (took away the main opportunity available to new migrants to better themselves)
- Slowing of post-World War II manufacturing (took away jobs)
- Community redlining (denied bank loans simply because one lived in a Black community)
- Numerous other forms of discrimination and happenings

The Black ghetto was being formed to cut successful Blacks and unsuccessful Blacks off from one another, setting the stage for the loss of reciprocity.

It is clear to see that, while the first Black migration was cohesive and had an agenda, the second migration was less educated and skilled. Thus, the North exploited them, and the first migration abandoned them. These circumstances, coupled with banks and other financial institutions not wanting to invest in these areas (redlining), segregation, and other factors set the formation of the Black urban ghetto into motion and created the isolation necessary to severely impact the reciprocity necessary for healthy Black love.

For the first time in American history, the Black community was isolated from one another. The first migration was isolated into pockets of educated Blacks chasing the American middle-class ideal alone (mental isolation) while the second migration was isolated into urban ghettos built to contain, miseducate, and exploit them (mental and physical isolation). The isolation that Blacks who migrated north experienced and felt eventually trickled down into the Black relationship and robbed it of its reciprocity.

To understand what isolation does to reciprocity, one must understand the psychological impact that isolation can have on an individual. Isolation can make a person feel as if he or she has to depend on himself or herself and look out for number one. Individuality becomes central and important to a person. Isolation can assist a person in forgetting about the responsibility he or she has to others because others have not looked out for him or her. A survival-of-the-fittest mentality takes over, which can kill reciprocity. When a relationship loses reciprocity, its members lose the motivation to share themselves, not just things. Sharing of the self is essential to any healthy relationship, especially a love relationship.

We can see this play itself out in movies like *ATL*, where a young, wealthy African American teenage girl feels socially isolated in her all-white community. She wants to be around other Black teenagers like herself, but, because her community does not have many, she is forced to go the "hood" to hang out with Black kids. Many successful Blacks complain about this isolation and being stuck in a world that does not accept them because they are Black. However, being poor and growing up in the "hood" can be just as lonely and isolating. Just like the actors in the movie, this has an effect on the love relationships of everyday Black people as well. The effects of isolation are reflected in one very powerful way, loneliness.

Loneliness is usually a consequence of isolation. It stems from a sense of not belonging. Everyone needs people around him or her to help, understand, and care for him or her. These are both psychological and spiritual necessities that reciprocity provides and isolation and loneliness destroy. The feeling of intimacy that reciprocity provides is essential to any relationship. Reciprocity provides the safety that relationship intimacy needs. Feelings of isolation break down that safety and make intimacy impossible.

We are specifically talking about the type of loneliness that affects the souls of Black folk. Loneliness of the soul is affecting African American relationships today, and it stems from this period. It has caused a form of alienation. This alienation that Black people feel toward one another in our love relationships originate from these migrations northward and the resulting disconnections that occurred between us as a people. The reason this caused the loss of reciprocity is simple. Reciprocity is something that has to be practiced within all aspects of one's life. It cannot be turned on and off. You cannot be reciprocal to your wife and kids, but look down and be selfish toward your neighbor and not think this behavior will seep into your love relationship. Your sense of isolation and feelings of alienation will flow into all your relationships because our ancestral lineage and linked fate connects us all. This is why reciprocity is so important. We are connected to one another as people of African descent. Reciprocity dictates we acknowledge this fact by behaving in a manner that fosters sharing and caring, or our relationships will suffer. The seeds of this suffering were laid during the great Black migrations to the promised land.

The Problem of Reciprocity and the Black Relationship

The loss of reciprocity trickled down into our relationships with one another. With the loss of reciprocity, it caused us to lose our responsibility to one another. No longer did we look out for each other's sisters or made sure our neighbor's husband got a job at the local shipping yard. Everyone began looking out for himself or herself, and this had devastating consequences for the Black relationship.

What responsibility do men have to women? What responsibility do women have to men? We never really think about these questions, but we should. In figuring out the answer, we begin to realize why we have lost some love for each other. In his documentary about his life, *A*

Great and Mighty Walk, Dr. John Henrik Clarke talked about the high
level of respect that men had for women during his time. When a man
and a woman were scheduled for a date, he would dress in his finest
clothes, meet her parents, and show her a respectable good time. He
did not need a lot of money. All he needed was to be a gentleman and
respectful. The same went for sisters. They were not trying to financially sum up a man. Rather, they took time to learn who he really was
and judged him based on some solid criteria.

As a man or woman, you knew you could not just mistreat or
abuse the opposite sex without someone knowing about it and seeing
you about it. The Black Panthers often talked about how they visited
men in the community who beat their wives and let them know
it wasn't cool to do it and it would be in their best interest if they
stopped. Everyone was accountable and responsible to each other in
the community.

Today, this does not happen. The reliance and cooperation we had
to develop during the nadir period evaporated during the migration
because Black folks began to distance themselves from other Black
folks. Don't we hear this same narrative today? How many times have
we heard various Black folks say things like, "When Hip-Hop artists
say 'bitch' or 'ho' in a song, they not talking about me." In truth, they
are talking about you. We, as Black folks, are linked and connected.
When one portion of our community is hurting, we all hurt. When
one segment of our community is insulted, we all should feel it. When
one segment of our communal family is doing wrong, we must all
hold them accountable and not be apathetic.

Let's think about why we distance ourselves from each other. It's
sometimes about education. Some Black folks are newly educated
while others aren't. This can create tension. We also distance ourselves
from each other because of skin color. Lighter-skinned Blacks sometimes receive more privilege in society than darker-skinned Blacks
do. This can cause resentment. Sometimes, it is class. Some say that
is what the Bill Cosby controversy represented, a highly successful
African American man criticizing low-income African American

families for their struggles, which stem from systemic factors. The unspoken tension between the Black poor and the Black middle class is a growing narrative in contemporary Black America. Still, it might be generational. Hip- Hop often becomes the vehicle through which to express and debate the growing divide between young and older Black folks. Whatever the perceived tension is, it distracts us from truly building strong and healthy communities that can help the vast majority of us. Division stops us from building strong and healthy families and relationships that are filled with love.

This blatant disregard for each other has made it possible for brothers and sisters to disrespect one another and think it is okay. It is not. The value that kept our communities and relationships in line was reciprocity. It kept us from disrespecting each other. It was a method of self-governance. For example, consider when a man or woman cheats on his or her spouse. The other person, if he or she were practicing community reciprocity, would not be a willing party to that act and would say, "Go home to your spouse. I am not going to assist in the destruction of a Black family because that hurts my community." Now since we have little reciprocity, it's a free-for-all. Reciprocity is a very important and essential concept. It is needed in order for us to get our relationships back together. Our lives cannot be about separating ourselves from each other. They need to be about developing healthy and positive relationships that will help us heal our communities.

Being in a loving and healthy Black relationship is our opportunity to share our love, joy, and happiness with each other. Too much of our time has been spent on distancing ourselves from each other. In sharing, we find we feel more fulfilled. Our love is our ultimate gift to each other. It is our chance to make our communities whole again and be accountable to ourselves and our fellow brothers and sisters. Only when we practice reciprocity do we begin to see our worlds filled with abundance, creativity, and possibility.

Promised Land?

Oh promised land, promised land,
Looking forward to my pot of American gold.

Oh promised land, promised land,
I left my family and land to go north because of
the hope and possibility I was sold.

Oh promised land, promised land,
I want to escape the violence and segregation of the
Southern white man.

Oh promised land, promised land,
Want to put down roots, start a family, and hopefully own
my piece of American land.

Oh promised land, promised land,
I have such big plans and big dreams about the big
city that I can hardly wait.

Oh promised land, promised land,
Let me go. I hear my train. I know this will be great!

Inspiring times.

The Black Panthers founder, Huey Newton, together with admirers in 1971. Harker, Joseph. 2006. Loud, proud and black. New Statesman 135:40–41.

CHAPTER FIVE

EYES ON THE PRIZE, BUT NOT ON LOVE: THE PROBLEM OF BALANCE

"This is the twenty-seventh time I have been arrested, and I ain't going to jail no more! The only way we gonna stop them white men from whuppin' us is to take over. What we gonna start sayin' now is Black Power!"

Kwame Toure (Stokely Carmichael)

"Discrimination is a hellhound that gnaws at Negroes in every waking moment of their lives to remind them that the lie of their inferiority is accepted as truth in the society dominating them."

Dr. Martin Luther King Jr.

"Love doesn't ask family members to choose."

Reverend Otis Moss III,
pastor of Trinity United Church of
Christ in Chicago

While attending service at Trinity Church one Sunday, we were privileged enough to be present to hear a sermon by Reverend Otis Moss, who was responding to the recent controversy and propaganda surrounding retired pastor Reverend Jeremiah Wright and then-Democratic presidential candidate Barack Obama. Reverend Moss was profound in his assessment of the situation. His message to the congregation was simple, "Love doesn't ask family members to choose."

The weight of his statement stuck with us as we drove home that Sunday. Love doesn't ask family members to choose. Reverend Moss was obviously speaking directly to our congregation, letting us know that it was okay to love both our brothers and support both of them, even if they were unfortunately at odds at the moment. We love them both, and we will not choose between them. Both of them have served the African American community and done much for this country. We will not and should not choose.

However, his statement also had us thinking about our book. It specifically had us reflecting on this chapter, which focuses on the Civil Rights/Black Power era and love. Reverend Moss' words also spoke to the danger that is inherent in all choice. You see, whenever you choose between things, you are setting up a hierarchy, privileging one thing over another, focusing on one thing more than another, and implicitly declaring something more important than another. This usually means that one thing gets your attention while the other gets discarded or at least neglected. During the Civil Rights movement and Black Power era, progress, freedom, and justice became the focus while other things were neglected.

This was a very difficult chapter for us to write because we have a lot of reverence, respect, and love for this era and the people who lived it. Taking a critical look at it brought us a great deal of discomfort. It was hard. We are here living the lives we live because of Dr. Martin Luther King Jr., Malcolm X, Dr. John Henrik Clarke, Amiri Baraka, SNCC, SCLC, NAACP, CORE, Kwame Toure, the Black Panther Party, Dr. Karenga, and others. We have been taught by, sat down with, and listened to numerous figures and elders from this era. Believe us when we say Akilah and Kamau are who they are because of who our elders were. We live by the African proverb, "A person is a person because there are people." We believe in this and teach our son this. The elders sacrificed for us and knocked down doors for us. They are a major reason why we are successful today, so it was difficult to look at a time in American history where Black people were so powerful mentally, socially, and intellectually and ask, "What about love? What part of the Black revolution talked about brothers and sisters loving each other and building strong and healthy families?" However, we felt it was necessary to really look at this pivotal time in history, analyze how love was discussed, and attempt to understand the ramifications for our relationships today. Just know that it was tough and done with love.

The Civil Rights and Black Power Era

People like Marcus Garvey, W.E.B Du Bois, Booker T. Washington, Martin Delany, Sojourner Truth, David Walker, and Fredrick Douglass laid the antecedent to the Civil Rights and Black Power era revolution. These icons helped shape the early consciousness necessary for revolution; so, when the disrespect and oppression of Blacks in America had come to a boil, we had narratives and blueprints to pull from to move forward. And move we did!

The Civil Rights and Black Power era in this country was an amazing time. It was a time ripe with possibility for change and pregnant with opportunity for many.

The Black Power movement (and the Civil Rights Movement for that matter) would launch a radical political movement that, while racially specific, was nevertheless interpreted by a variety of multiracial groups as a template for restructuring society (Joseph, 2007).

There has never been a more powerful movement before or since for change in their country. Around the world, various people have consistently re-created and used this era to bring about political change. It cannot be understated enough that life for Black people would look radically different today if it were not for this time and the courage of many from this era.

The recognized time period of this particular era is 1955 to 1968 for the Civil Rights movement and 1966 to 1975 for the Black Power era. These movements were aimed at ending racial discrimination and restoring African American citizenship and enhancing Black pride. The time period was a point in American history where Black opposition to white domination and supremacy were collectively taken up by the Black community. We say "collectively" because pockets of resistance have always existed in the Black community since we first set foot on American soil. However, this period represented a point of collective cohesion against the forces that sought to keep Black people poor and powerless.

This movement was responsible for numerous notable legislative achievements, such as the Civil Rights Acts of 1964 and 1968, Voting Rights Act, desegregation, Black Is Beautiful movement, affirmative action, and Immigration and Nationality Act. These and other societal changes were brought about through a variety of strategies from civil resistance to overtly defiant opposition. These included sit-ins, voter registration, marches, boycotts, uprising, speeches, rallies, debates, armed protection, and, at times, violent defense.

We are presenting this chapter as if the Black Power and Civil Rights movements go together, but, as most know, this was not a monolithic time for Black people. Even though both movements influenced one another (and needed one another), there was still an internal struggle within the African American community for the hearts and minds of Black folk, especially the youth, between the two ideologies.

While Black people were making a choice between the two ideological revolutionary ways of thinking, they were simultaneously being pushed to subconsciously make other choices because of the times. Black men and women were implicitly choosing between two equally important emotional states, being strong or nurturing love. Because of the constitution, we needed to change American society. Strength won, and, unfortunately, love lost.

The Problem of Balance

During this time period, Black people were changing the world. This was a time of great turmoil and challenge within the Black community. However, it was also a time of internal reflections, changes, and choices for our community. You see, revolution is difficult. It's hard. Changing the world requires you change yourself. Sometimes, the changes you have to make, while they may help you get the job done, have severe consequences for your personal life. Sometimes, the price of progress, especially difficult progress, can be the sacrifice of your family life. Ask any very successful businessperson how challenging it is to balance professional achievement and family issues, and he or she will tell you that it's extremely difficult. Now take that scenario, multiply it by a thousand times, and make it collective. Then you have the massive challenge facing the Black community during this period. It is safe to say that the emphasis and focus during this period was more on progress of the Black family than on healing the Black family. Revolution demanded the development of a particular type of emotional constitution necessary for battle.

During the Civil Rights and Black Power era, Black people had to be very strong. They had to manifest a type of energy that was about strength, battle, and struggle. Even the Civil Rights movement, though a nonviolent resistance, still required participants to be strong and ready for battle. This strong persona that Black people had no choice but to adopt solidified a character type that was already floating around the Black community historically, and this made it the norm. So the strong Black man and strong Black woman archetype took center stage within the Black relationship.

We are all familiar with friends and family within the Black community who call themselves "strong Black men" and "strong Black women." If you are like us, you probably never question where this type of talk comes from. However, we began to question the origins of this type of narrative and believe, while it was not originated in this time period, it was definitely utilized more here than at any other time in Black American history. At this time, African Americans needed to feel, act, and present strong images if things were going to change for us in this country. Others were watching and looking for reasons to deny us rights. Part of their argument was that Blacks were not smart enough to warrant freedom. So many of our champions of the time went about the task of trying to prove people wrong, but, in the process, they may have neglected some of the important emotional work we had to do within our own families. We accentuated the strong part of who we were while downplaying our vulnerability and sensitivity. After a while, we started acting like this with not only others, but with each other as well. This caused the loss of balance between Black men and women.

One of our mentors once asked us, "What would Black relationships look like if Black people didn't have to struggle and fight for equality within their entire time in this county?" We couldn't answer the question. Then an even more poignant question was asked. What would your relationship look like? We are still contemplating our answer. The point is that something has to give. To be strong Black men and women, we had to be totally focused on strength. Family issues had to take a backseat for progress to be made. A strong front had to be fortified. There was no room for vulnerability. Consequently, the balance in our families suffered.

Balance was affected because two people attempting to show their strength are not able to easily transition to an equally important aspect of a relationship, sensitivity, and vulnerability. Therefore, the relationship is thrown out of balance. The relationship becomes more of a struggle or test of wills rather than a caring and loving journey. Every disagreement becomes a fight; every affront becomes a platform to show how strong and powerful one is. Relationships are about compromise and being able to be vulnerable. Compromise preserves balance. The strife between Black men and Black women got wider during this time because everyone was trying to gain more power. Some brothers felt like sisters were part of the larger society and trying to oppress them. Some sisters felt like brothers were trying to lord over them and keep them in the kitchen. The fact of the matter is that we needed each other more during this time, not less. We progressed, but it sometimes felt like we progressed in two different directions.

Sometimes, Kamau defers to Akilah. Sometimes, based upon the context, timing, and severity of the situation, Akilah defers to Kamau. But we won't end up oppressing each other because we are working toward balance. However, balance is based on sensitivity and empathy. Unfortunately, these things disappear when you have two people who are attempting to show how strong and powerful they are. Within this context, balance becomes an impossibility.

The Significance of Balance

With balance comes relationship peace. That is not to say that your relationship won't experience problems or strife, but you will deal with it differently if you have balance. People often are amazed at the fact that we fight. They say, "You guys disagree on things." We look at them dumbfounded and say, "Hell yeah!" But these disagreements don't ever threaten our relationship because we have balance within our union. We can defer to one another when appropriate. We can disagree, argue, and stay on topic. We don't bring up situations that have already been resolved. We don't look to hurt one another because we have balance. In an argument, we aren't looking to win. Strong people are looking to win and show no weakness. We are looking to resolve the situation. We would much rather be happy than be always right. This means putting our individual egos aside and working together as one. This is the gift that balance brings to a relationship. We always try to be even-keeled and levelheaded. Balance ensures you aren't living in the past or focused on the future at the expense of the present.

Balance is the point where two people meet and establish equilibrium, a sort of relationship homeostasis that they can always come back to and pull from when things get rough within the relationship. Obstacles and disruptions become minor occurrences when relationship balance is established. In fact, when balance exists, you are aware that bad times will develop within a relationship, but good times will follow. Therefore unrealistic expectations are never developed. You will be able to ride out the tough times in anticipation of the good. You will be able to relish the good times, but simultaneously understand that adversity is coming. When it comes, it won't shatter your fairy-tale beliefs about love because you won't have any. There is another word for balance, and it's called understanding.

Our elders within this time period gave up balance for the sake of progress. They gave up balance for us so we could have a better society and, ultimately, more freedom to live, enjoy life and cultivate understanding in a more peaceful environment than they had. Unfortunately, Black relationships still suffer from the strong syndrome and the subsequent imbalance that flows from it. So, questions remain:

- What does being a strong Black man or woman mean for your relationship?
- What would your relationship look like if we didn't have to struggle as a people?
- Is there balance within your union?

Think before you answer because these questions just might save your relationship!

Where's the Love?

One of the greatest tragedies of this era was that, in our effort to achieve our civil rights in America, our struggle didn't include a solid discussion of the Black family and Black love. During the time, Whitney M. Young stated, "The Black family was a peripheral issue" within the Civil Rights movement (Lemann, 1992). Very little focus was placed on the family and how it was rapidly changing and affecting millions of African Americans. The Black family saw some of its most dramatic change during this time. Fewer fathers were home, more women were having babies by themselves, and African American urban poverty and isolation skyrocketed. This was the time when the black middle class was abandoning many of our neighborhoods for better opportunities and low-income Blacks were being contained within large housing projects. Because Black folks had to develop the picture-perfect image of the Black family in the minds of white people, in order to achieve equality in America, we couldn't deal with the issues that were occurring within our low-income communities. Young and some other civil rights leaders at that time believed it would be dangerous to address the internal issues happening in many low-income Black communities because of how the opponents to the Civil Rights movement might perceive and use it. There was no space in the struggle to talk about and strengthen Black love and families.

So much about the Civil Rights and Black Power era was focused on preserving the image of the African American family, and it was for good reason. Before the Civil Rights and Black Power movements, Blacks were seen as inferior and socially dysfunctional, so we don't blame many of the leaders of the time for not fully addressing what was happening with the Black family. After all, more than 50 percent of African American families at the time had a mother and father at home and were considered intact. The Black middle class was growing due to the manufacturing industry, government jobs, and increased education, but issues remained. The problems happening in the Black family today are related to the occurrences of the past. During the mid-to late-1960s, 50 percent of African American children were born to two parents. Today, that number is 31 percent and dropping every year. Trying to be strong and exude a false image of the Black family hurt us because these practices didn't give us any space to be vulnerable, heal, and strengthen our family relationships. We weren't able to focus on our family and rebuild what American racism stripped away. Today, we have children growing up who haven't seen married parents for two and three generations. How can we expect to promote healthy marriages if people rarely see them? Where do you learn to be in a lasting relationship? The *Washington Post* published an article about the perception of marriage by Black youth. What they found was that since many Black youth have not seen a healthy marriage, they feel it is something that only white people do. "Black people don't get married," said an eighth-grade student. We must reverse this belief!

Akilah has been lucky. She is one of the 31 percent of African American children who has seen a loving, healthy marriage. Her parents have been married for thirty-six years. She is quick to tell people that having that model in her life has made a tremendous difference in her relationships. Like everything else that one is successful in life at, marriage is work, commitment, and dedication. Akilah has received a firsthand view of what that looks like. It is important that we help our young people understand that marriage is a viable and important option for them in the future. Making a long-term commitment is one of the most fulfilling life choices you can make. However, to teach our young people this, we must change our own views toward marriage and relationships and be serious about creating strong and productive marriages. We must deal with the strong Black man and strong Black woman identities we have.

The family will always be central to healthy communities. You can't have a thriving healthy community without vibrant and healthy families. The Civil Rights and Black Power movements weren't merely about progressing; they were about progressing together as Black men and women. Remember, when the Europeans came to Africa and captured Africans, the first thing they did to weaken our power was to separate the men and women. That is what is happening today. Strong Black men and strong Black women, separated from one another.

Letter to our mothers and fathers

Dear Mothers and Fathers,

I just wanted to say thank you for all your sacrifice, courage and social consciousness. You had the insight to say to white supremacy, hell No! You said no to racism. You said no to oppression and you said no to the status quo. Your uncompromising movement laid the groundwork for the changes of today. I appreciate your willingness to die for what you believed in. Because without that type of unwavering dedication, I couldn't enjoy the freedoms I do today. The books you wrote, the poems you composed, the protests you led, the programs you started, and yes the blood you shed was like my north star to liberation.

I don't pretend to understand the types of comforts you had to relinquish for revolution to come to America. All I can say is that without you there is no me. There is no Jabari, so for that I can't express the gratitude I feel. And, don't worry. We are going to get the things fixed in the community that need to be fixed. You did not revolt in vain.

Finally, I just want to say that whenever someone says I can't do something or when people attempt to oppress me because all they see is a body and don't recognize the soul which resides within, I think of you and I receive the strength to keep moving. I remember the legacy of power you left me and I handle my business the way I know you would have.

So no matter whether your motto was "power to the people" or "we shall overcome."

I thank you for your struggle, and won't stop fighting, until justice has won!

Sincerely

Akilah

CHAPTER SIX

FREE LOVE: THE PROBLEM OF UNITY AND COMMON PURPOSE

"Freedom is not free. Freedom is something you take with your own hands. You maintain it with your own hands. Freedom is not handed down from one generation to another. Each generation must assume the responsibility of securing their manhood and womanhood."

Dr. John Henrik Clarke

"Our first mistake was that we thought of freedom as a place, rather than as a continuation of a struggle. Tyranny never sleeps. Our second mistake was that we thought of freedom as a goal, rather than as a launching pad from which to reach our goals. Without purpose, freedom hardly matters. Our third mistake was that we thought that freedom made us free. That, however, is license, not freedom at all. Freedom is being shackled to identity, purpose, and direction and being in constant pursuit."

Asa G. Hilliard III

O NE of our favorite documentaries, along with *500 Years Later* by Halaqah Films, is the HBO film, *The Bastards of the Party*. This tremendous piece of work depicts the origins, rise, and solidification of Black street gangs in the Los Angeles area. We think this documentary does an excellent job of showing what has occurred in our inner cities post-Civil Rights and Black Power era. It accurately displays the enormous obstacles, both historical and contemporary, that our African American urban youth have to avoid and conquer in order to succeed. However, we think it also does an excellent job of capturing the post-Civil Right challenges that Black love has had to contend with. Forces such as drugs, Black male unemployment, Reaganomics, and the loss of leadership have all proven to be great obstacles to the Black community and have helped facilitate the loss of unity within our own love relationships.

What Happened to Black Power and the Dream?

After the Civil Rights and the Black Power era, Blacks made great strides in education, business, economic attainment, and political power. African Americans were achieving the American dream of home ownership and middle-class status like never before. Along with the 1968 Fair Housing Act, affirmative action programs, and influx of African Americans working for the state and federal government, many African Americans were achieving unprecedented levels of financial security and mobility. But many African Americans were left behind. The great opportunities didn't happen for all Blacks. A large percentage found only further hardship, American discrimination, and urban community decay. The reasons for these hardship are numerous and important to this next chapter in the African American love story. The Black community was in a state of disarray of sorts as it looked for definition. Some of the causes for this difficult time are outlined in the pages that follow.

The Void of Black Leadership

Anyone who knows anything about the Black community understands that African Americans greatly respect the Black leaders of the

1960s and early 1970s. These leaders are worthy of being honored
because they acted with conviction and valor in the defense of the
Black community as it pursued equal rights within this country. They
were (and are) symbols of hope, change, and possibility for millions of
Black people young and old. But others knew this as well and figured
the dismantling of this leadership would be the quickest way to derail
the great political and social changes that were taking place in America
during the 1960s and 1970s. If you couple this with the thinking of
many Americans that America had turned the corner in regards to race
relations, this made for a recipe of chaos and disunity.

The death, exile, discrediting or imprisonment of numerous Black
leaders such as Malcolm X, Martin Luther King Jr., Medgar Evers,
Asante Shakur, Fred Hampton, Huey P. Newton, and Bobby Hutton
created a sense of demoralization and disarray in the Black community and left a void within regular Black folk. With so much loss, a
people's hearts can become cynical and overburdened. The eradica-
tion of so many Black leaders over the years took its toll on the Black
community.

Post-Fordism

From the beginning of the 1920s until the late 1960s, many Black
communities formed themselves around assembly line-type factories
and industrialized companies. This was done to have close access to the
jobs these companies provided. This process was known as Fordism,
named after Henry Ford, the owner of Ford Motors. This assembly
line/specialized worker format was most associated with him and his
factories. For the Black community, in many instances, this just served
to reinforce the segregation and isolation that most African American
communities were already experiencing. However, it did serve as a
major source of income for the Black community at this time. We all
hear elders talk about Black communities being wonderful and vibrant
cities during the 1940s, 1950s, and 1960s. Many of these communities were able to have the economics they did have because Black

folks were working in these factories and earning a descent living. America was growing. Again, it needed Blacks to supply a great deal of its labor.

Unfortunately, this Fordism condition did not last forever. By the late 1960s and early 1970s, factories began relocating their operations, usually overseas. All over the country, jobs were disappearing, and factories were shutting down. The era of Post-Fordism was underway, ushered in by changes in the political climate, aspects of globalization, and a revolution in advanced technology. Post-Fordism completely changed the American workforce. Gone was the assembly-line worker. A new premium was placed on highly skilled individuals. Companies no longer needed specialized employees in bulk; workers with numerous technical skills were sought. Education became an even more important tool than ever before as companies focused on recruiting college-educated applicants while line workers and menial labor employees were devalued or dismissed altogether.

These developments hit the African American community especially hard. Already living in isolated and segregated communities, the loss of major employment centers was devastating. Throughout urban America, hard-working African American communities became many of the depressed urban areas you see today. Post-Fordism permanently changed the landscape of the Black community in many American cities.

Almost overnight, blue-collar, African American men who embodied the American work ethic became unemployed blights on society and a major problem within the Black community. This was exasperated further as African American women began to supplant Black men in the new technologically and educationally advanced workforce. Black women have always worked outside the home, but the jobs they were regulated to didn't disappear. The jobs that Black men relied upon did. Black women were still able to work, although they were menial domestic jobs. Brothers were being removed from the workforce altogether. This had devastating effects on marriage roles in the Black community. William Julius Wilson, a world-renowned sociologist, believed African American men have become unmarriage-able due to high levels of unemployment and very low wage jobs. He showed how income affects marriage rates among Black men. Wilson reported that, in 1987, 50 percent of African American men between the ages of eighteen and twenty-nine who had incomes over $20,000 were married. This is compared to only 39 percent for those with incomes between $15,000 and $20,000, 29 percent for those earning between $10,000 and $15,000, 7 percent for those earning between $1,000 and $5,000, and only 3 percent for those with no reported earnings (Wilson, 1997).

Original research conducted by Akilah Watkins-Butler using data from the University of Minnesota, the Integrated Public Use Microdata Series.

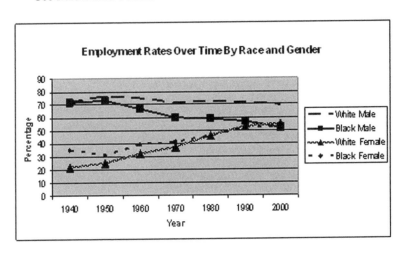

We are not saying that employment is the only factor in Black people getting married. We don't believe that. We believe there is a cumulative effect. Our entire history in America has contributed to why Black people struggle to love each other. The unemployment and underemployment of Black men is just one component.

Nevertheless, similar to many other times in American history, Black men were again being taught that they were less than. However, the unique aspect this time was that Black men couldn't turn to Black women for comfort or solace because the economic structure of the time made them competitors. Black women had jobs, but Black men didn't. Akilah remembers her father talking to her as she grew up about this dynamic in America. He said, "Akilah, you need to work and get things on your job like insurance for you and Kamau because the white man doesn't like giving a Black man a job with those kind of benefits." This kind of different treatment between Black men and Black women has caused a serious rift in the Black relationship.

The Black man's image has been severely damaged in his own eyes and, not to mention, in Black women's eyes. He has been left unemployed, underemployed, and struggling without a shoulder to cry on.

Neoliberalism

In 1973, the American political economy began to change in response to the growing oil crisis that was occurring throughout the world. A return to a freer and more self-reliant economic structure was being instituted. Everybody had to look out for himself or herself and his or her individual families. The safety net of government programs was disappearing. The country was returning to an economic political structure it knew very well. Its supporters argued the new system would be best for America and, if given a true chance to flourish, it would be successful. Neoliberals felt that, by forcing poor people into this new economic system, they would become more productive and add financially to America rather than take away. However, its detractors suggested it was a cold and uncaring structure that didn't take into account the needs of the most vulnerable among us. How were people without many historical opportunities economically going to take advantage of this new system without the necessary skills and education? Regardless of where one fell in the debate, the impending reality was clear. We were returning to a liberal economic structure called Neoliberalism.

Neoliberalism, or a free market economy, can be defined as the institution of a set of:

[T]axation structures that favor capital accumulation over income redistribution, industrial policies that minimize the presence of the state in private industry and the retrenchment of welfare spending (Prasad, 4).

Basically, it is to make as much money as possible, let the rich get richer, forget the poor, and cut many public programs. This move to a free market economy hit African American communities very hard because they were already reeling from Post-Fordism. Now a shift from governmental regulation and welfare spending to help the poor to an entrepreneurial and economic prosperity focus further crippled a community lacking economic capital. This is best crystallized by the 1980s, an era referred to by many as the reign of Reaganomics.

In America, the 1980s were a tumultuous time for African Americans. An already vulnerable Black community had the welfare state rolled back and many governmental programs cut while personal responsibility was passed to a predominantly ill-prepared community. Many urban African American communities were left to their own devices and to basically decay. Worse than that, Blacks were blamed for why their communities looked the way they did. It was definitely a time when you were expected to pull yourself up by your boot-straps. Unfortunately, because of historical oppression, many African American communities were left without boots.

African American males, still dealing with Post-Fordism unem-ployment and poor self-image, were now thrust into a political market where the strong survive and conquering the free market economy was the aim of the game. However, many Black men did not possess the economic capital or historical advantages to be competitive in the game, so many became perpetual losers and victims of the game. This created both shame in Black men and a loss of faith in Black relation-ships in Black women.

Neoliberalism withdrew the help that could have assisted many Black families and further exasperated the feelings of inferiority of Black men and resentment between Black men and women. The new measuring stick for what it meant to be a man was economic accumulation. Many Black men seemingly didn't measure up. This added to the feelings that many Black men had of powerlessness and insecurity.

The War on Drugs

During the 1980s and early 1990s, the United States was inundated with a serious crack cocaine epidemic. The circumstances of how the drugs were brought into the country and how they ended up predominately in the Black community are a topic for another book. Nevertheless, the crack cocaine epidemic and ensuing War on Drugs was a major negative development for the Black community and Black families.

The War on Drugs was a campaign intended to reduce the flow of drugs into American cities, specifically crack cocaine. Officially, it was "a set of laws and policies that were intended to discourage the production, distribution, and consumption of targeted substances" (Wikipedia, 2008) by using a complex mix of community policing, ad campaigns, foreign and domestic policy, and harsh drug laws. However, the results have been far from stellar. This war has resulted in the enactment of racially biased drugs laws, uneven sentencing, high recidivism rates, and stigmatization of the entire Black urban community.

The War on Drugs has in fact resulted in the creation of a permanent underclass of people who have few education or job opportunities, often as a result of being punished for drug offenses, which in turn have resulted from attempts to earn a living in spite of having no education or job opportunities (Wikipedia, 2008).

Eventually, the War on Drugs deteriorated into a war on the Black community and, effectively, a war on the Black male and Black family. It helped usher in an era of mass incarceration of Black males and created, defined, and solidified the perception of the Black man as a criminal. This image of Black men as criminals persists to this day. It is an image that every respectable brother has to negotiate with individuals who don't know him.

In an attempt to grasp some form of Neoliberal power and prosperity in a Post-Fordism society, some Black men turned to dealing drugs. However, all this did was lead to mass incarceration, which furthered the resentment between Black men and women by making Black men further unmarriageable in the minds of Black women and disconnecting Black men from the family. The influx of drugs into the Black community also assisted in the exploitation of Black women, who engaged in sexual activities to further their drug habit, and affected an entire generation of children within the Black family by destabilizing the people who care for them. With the mass incarceration of Black men and aforementioned residual effects of drugs, Black relationships suffered. Resentment and blame deepened, and unity was dealt a blow. This is a serious issue because unity is vital to the success of any relationship and community. It must be maintained at all cost.

With the institution of a new political economic structure, which valued money over people (Neoliberalism); fewer jobs and employment opportunities (Post-Fordism); and influx of drugs into many communities and subsequent War on Drugs, which incarcerated numerous African males, things got worse for Black love.

The Problem of Unity

Now the beginning of this chapter might suggest the disarray and chaos caused by the above factors led to the problem of unity. This might be true in some sense, but we feel a more significant occurrence that led to the problem of unity was the development of intense resentment between Black men and women. Post-Fordism and Neoliberalism opened and poured salt into a wound that already existed. Remember, Black men and women never received the peace needed to love each other. These economic systems drove a further wedge between brothers and sisters. This was the true obstacle to the unity needed for Black love. Where there is resentment, unity becomes an increasingly difficult thing to obtain or hold together.

Historical obstacles during this time period hit the African American community hard. A collection of unfortunate events happened one after another. The first problem was the death and jailing of African American leaders, leaving the community without many of the leaders they had grown to love and respect, which created a kind of anger, resentment, and frustration within the community. This anger and frustration was redirected and trickled down to those closest to you. In this case, it was your loved ones. We have seen cases of this throughout Black history in this country where angered and frustrated African Americans have taken to the streets and turned their displeasure with American society on the only thing they had access to, their own communities and families. Another example of this behavior would be African American gangs. Many of which started out as protection against roving white gangs that would infiltrate the Black community and look to hurt African Americans. They take the anger and frustration they have from the lack of employment opportunity, quality education, and economic prosperity within their communities and turn the rage they feel on their own communities and families. If you are a psychoanalyst, you call this "displacement," the redirecting of anger and rage you feel for another person or situation toward a more accessible and weaker target. Basically, it is being angry with your boss and kicking your dog when you get home. Joy Leary, author of *Post Traumatic Slave Syndrome*, calls this "killing the part of you that isn't loved." The anger Black people feel for not being appreciated within American society is turned inward toward themselves and their community. We feel a similar thing occurred during this time period. The anger that Black people felt from the unfairness of the systematic death and imprisonment of its leadership was turned inward toward those closest to us, that is, ourselves. This laid the seeds that made resentment between Black men and women possible.

After the death and jailing of many Black leaders happened, then Post-Fordism occurred, which caused many Black men to lose their jobs and only source of income to take care of their families. However, more importantly, Post-Fordism switched the needs of the workforce. Employment went from a very specialized factory setting that stereotypically favored men in general to a technically skilled office enterprise that stereotypically favored women. It is important to understand that Black women have always worked, but now, with the switch in the composition of the workforce, there was increased opportunity for them and decreased opportunity for Black men. The mass unemployment of Black men and growing employment and subsequent education of Black women caused resentments between African American men and women that are felt to this day.

Exasperating the growing resentment between Black men and women was the shift in the political economy. Neoliberalism changed the very definition of what it meant to be a man and a human being in society. It told individuals that their self-worth was tied to their economic earning potential and shifted what it meant to be a good father and husband. Gone were the days of *Leave It to Beaver* or *Good Times*, where being a good father meant being understanding, caring, and a disciplinarian. Now, your worth as a man, father, or husband was linked to you being a good earner and economically stable. If you aren't, you are not a man or marriageable partner. It amazes us every time we hear Black people say that Black men are not marriageable. That is why only 31 percent of our children are raised in two-parent households, which has been shown to produce excellent outcomes in various developmental, emotional, and academic domains for children. This belief of Black men being unmarriageable is based upon a Neoliberal understanding of society. When you look at the educational statistics in this country, it is clear that we are poorly educating and stigmatizing African American males at all levels. Teacher bias, low expectations, academic tracking, inadequate funding, subpar

instruction, stereotyping, special education, behavior disorder diag-
noses, and unfair suspension and expulsion are all disproportionately
affecting African American males. Economic attainment later in life
is directly connected to academic achievement early in life. So, if we
know this, then why do we continue to blame Black men for not
being marriageable? This only causes Black men to react with, "Black
women are not holding us down. They are selfish." This only further
deepens resentment between Black men and women. A more productive strategy would be to know that any relationship will take some
work. We should look to build upon the strengths of our partner, not
upon the resentment for what he or she does not have.

Our relationship is a perfect example of this. Kamau may be at the
University of Chicago now, but he had significant credit, debt, employment, and academic issues when we met. Like some of our brothers,
he became disillusioned with college and felt like it wasn't giving him
the appropriate information. He was working two menial jobs that
weren't leading to any real advancement, and he wasn't getting his
life moving anywhere. Many would say he wasn't marriageable. Why
date him? But we worked as a team, and that is what marriage and
love is about, working together for the betterment of the union. Fast-
forward seven years later, he has three degrees and working toward
a PhD at one of the most illustrious universities in the world. He is
one-half of a very successful marriage, an important and inspirational
part of Akilah's life, and an excellent father. If Akilah had held onto a
Neoliberal definition of what a man should be, none of this happiness
would have occurred.

Akilah has often said that many of her sisters complain about not
meeting a good Black guy, but they don't realize that there are many
good Black guys around if they are willing to look. Many sisters want a
man who is already successful and ready-made. While living in Atlanta,
we knew many sisters who drove expensive cars, lived in huge five-
bedroom houses, and worked very prestigious jobs. However, many
of them are alone, and it isn't because they are successful. Successful
Black women are not alone because they are successful and their

achievements threaten Black men. That is another myth and false-hood meant to keep us apart. The true problem is that many women want an ideal man who is perfect, good-looking, wealthy, and college-educated. They also want a man with a great job, great credit and performs well in bed. This is unrealistic. Unrealistic expectations are killing Black relationships. One of Akilah's friends once said, "I don't want to grow with anyone. I spent too much time working on myself. Don't I deserve a man who is on my level or higher?" Our reply is that you may be in denial about the position and dilemma America has left Black people in. Hopefully, this book will clearly show that what we see in our current relationships isn't something that just happened. It has been a devastating progression. Walking away from each other, especially when we need each other the most, is not the answer. What you currently see in a potential partner may not reflect his or her true possibilities. Sisters and brothers must work with one another, not against each other. The basic structure of American society makes this an inescapable necessity.

The Power of Unity

Love and freedom require constant work. Love and freedom are not a place or a destination. They entail being engaged in a continuous struggle for happiness. However, this struggle will lead to numerous benefits along the way. Talib Kweli said Black love is a beautiful struggle, as it should be. However, unity is essential and necessary to this process. There is power in unity. If you lose unity within your relationship, you lose a bit of the transformative power in your life. Ayi Kwei Armah said, "All beauty is in the creative power of our rela-tionships." Armah didn't say some beauty is. He said all beauty is. We cannot achieve things in this world by ourselves. Whether it is academic, business, or political success, it requires the collective and unified efforts and support of many. No one achieves alone. There is no more powerful and creative union than the love relationship between a man and a woman.

In considering the importance of unity, let's think about it physically. We are all here because of the union between a man and woman. Without this form of physical unity, the greatest creation, life, cannot occur. If we think about it psychologically, the best decisions and most psychologically healthy people are able to strike a unity between logic and emotion. Further, let's look at it from a happiness standpoint. The happiest people are usually those able to strike a unity between their professional and personal lives. The point is that unity matters, and it matters to relationships as well. When you come together with another person, you are able to form something greater than yourself that you can then use to conquer all obstacles in your life. One cannot survive or thrive on one's own. Therefore, life requires and demands unity. Love does, too.

By becoming unified, we are presented with the opportunity to see life and all its possibilities. To heal the pain and rift between Black men and women, we need to move closer together, not further apart. In our closeness and love, we will begin to transcend our circumstances. Our relationships, if healthy, have tremendous healing power. Love has the power to birth something that wasn't there before, that is, something that is powerful and beneficial for ourselves as well as our community. It is not too late for us. We are at a point that offers many possibilities for loving each other. By becoming more loving toward ourselves and each other, we begin to tap into a great potential for change, a change that can lead us to shape a new vision for the Black family and community.

Dreams

We have lost so much, but still here I stand.
I stand with knowledge in my head
and my pride in my hand.
I scream, "Black is beautiful,"
and the masses seem to finally understand.
However, those with ill intent still
show their displeasure for my new found brand.
They have stacked the deck
and made my liberation a task seemingly all too grand.
They have taken away jobs, services, and opportunity
and attacked my newfound unity with impunity.
They have turned my plans into dreams unheard,
and we all know what happens to a dream deferred!

CHAPTER SEVEN

UMMA DO ME (WHAT'S GOING ON NOW): THE PROBLEM OF SACRIFICE

"You make it sprinkle/I make it tsunami/You get chump change/ But I get money!"

Rocko, Hip-Hop artist

"Verily, verily, I say unto you, except a grain of wheat fall into the ground and die, it abideth alone, but if it die, it bringeth forth much fruit."

Holy Bible

For those of you who see the quotes and picture and believe this chapter is going to be about Hip- Hop's influence on Black America and relationships or some perceived culture of disrespect, we are sorry, but we might disappoint you. Plenty of books, articles, and popular forms of media take up this subject, most notably the work of Bakari Kitwana, author of *The Hip-Hop Generation*. Instead, we are going to address a more implicit and hidden factor affecting contemporary Black love, which we feel has significantly affected the value of sacrifice, the problem of self-centeredness.

I'm Doin' Me

At this moment, we would like to ask you how often do you stress or focus on the "I." How regularly do you separate yourself out from others as special or better? Do you often find yourself saying things like, "I got to look out for me and mines," or "I did this by hard work and perseverance," or "I don't have time to take care of someone else. I gotta do me." The importance here is the "I." Understanding how that little letter shapes everything is necessary to comprehending what we are saying. When asked about how it felt to be the first African American presumptive nominee for president, Barack Obama promptly said he stood on the backs of others before him who paved the way. When asked how it felt to be the first African American coach to win the Super Bowl, Tony Dungy quickly stated he was indebted to those Black coaches who came before him. No "I." No "I did this by myself." No self-centeredness. This may not seem like a big deal, but it is. Our language can influence our thinking about reality, thus shaping our reality.

This type of "I" thinking comes directly from the Neoliberal orientation discussed previously. Too often, people quickly realize that the amount of money they can obtain or generate usually define their worth. This has caused people to not want to be associated with anyone who they feel can't benefit them. Building something with someone from the ground up has become taboo. Investing in someone (other than youth) has become unheard of. We are in the era of everyone wanting to get put on. Everyone is asking, "What's in it for me?" Everyone is hustling, grinding, making money, and degrading the next person who doesn't have as much and being extremely braggadocios. And please don't think it's just Black youth or Hip-Hop artists. How many times have you gone to a party and been bombarded with numerous business cards, business ideas, and networking opportunities? Now, don't be mislead. We understand the importance of networking and connecting with people, but what happened to the days when people just got to know one another on a human level or when people asked you how you were doing and really cared about your answer? Hopefully, with the new presidential administration's focus on service, teamwork, and togetherness, this situation will change.

In terms of dating and relationships, it now seems you aren't getting to know someone. It's like you are on a job interview, running down your résumé or curriculum vitae for people, so they can make a decision on whether to employ you as their boyfriend or girlfriend. If that works out, then they'll commit to a long-term partnership called marriage. If not, you are banished to the bad investment pile. Akilah has friends who won't date a guy unless they receive a full credit report by the third date. They explain, "There is no reason to invest your time in someone who you can't marry. I want a house and a nice car so I can't waste my time with someone who can't get that stuff." Look, we live in the world just like everyone else and understand the importance of achieving financial prosperity. But damn! People are so much deeper than a credit score or a limit. All this causes the loss of sacrifice, which is essential in maintaining a long and healthy relationship.

The Self-centered Wars

Most long-term relationships break up for three major reasons: money, emotional distance, and infidelity. All three share something in common. They are often the result of self-centeredness on the part of an individual involved in the relationship. Now, we are not saying that all self-centeredness is bad. Sometimes, you need to be self-centered in order to overcome a personal problem. For instance, a women who has been violated definitely needs time to emotionally and physically heal from the attack and requires as much self-centered time as is necessary to recover. Further, a man who has lost his job and is economically strapped needs as much self-centered time as he can muster to plan out his next move. However, these and other understandable situations aside, there are times when self-centeredness can destroy a relationship.

118 KAMAU AND AKILAH BUTLER

Money Matters

Sharing money with someone is a very intimate and sensitive thing. It is not just two people coming together around money. It is really two families with ways of handling money coming together. Most of us get our dealings with money from our parents. How they thought about and handled money is probably how we will. If two people come together with different familial ways of handling money, there inevitably will be some friction.

We definitely have different thoughts around money. Kamau is more freewheeling, and Akilah is more frugal. Early in our relationship, it was difficult coming to a common ground. There were arguments and disagreements, but we worked it out.

However, the task of coming together around economics is made extremely more difficult if parties act in a self-centered manner. The discussion of shared money and family economics takes understanding regarding how your partner may have grown up around money. Being self-centered negates and minimizes the way your mate deals with money, and this will cause resentment, hurt feelings, and eventually fights as each person seeks dominance over the couple's finances. One person will be seen as selfish while the other is seen as a liability.

Emotional Distance

Emotional distance is really about distrust. When a person is emotionally distant in a relationship, it conveys to his or her partner that, "I don't fully trust you with my feelings, and I am being self-centered with my emotions." It says, "I am hiding my true self from you." Nothing builds resentment in a relationship more than the withholding of intimacy. Think about it. We get into long-term relationships and marriage because we want closeness with another person. If this was not the case, we would just have sexual fling after fling. If the emotional closeness isn't there, it defeats the purpose of the relationship. The relationship loses its meaning in a way. The partners in the relationship are reduced to two people who live together rather than two people who love one another. If you are doing this, please stop. Face your fears and share them with your loved one before it's too late.

Infidelity

The epitome of self-centeredness is infidelity. If self-centeredness was a mountain, then infidelity would be its peak. Infidelity conveys to your partner that you don't care about his or her feelings. It is the ultimate violation. It speaks volumes. It says, "You thought I was in this relationship with you, but I've really been about me for some time now." It also communicates a supreme dissatisfaction with the relationship to your partner and can usually be the deathblow to the relationship. However, the most devastating thing about infidelity, other than the lies that usually accompany it, is the hard pill to swallow that it represents to your partner. It tells them, "There is someone in this world that I find more desirable than you." Now, people aren't dumb. They know there is always someone in the world who is prettier, bigger, better-dressed, more popular, and so forth. But what makes people comfortable in marriage is the beautiful notion of "This person chose me. This person loves me enough to spend his or her life with me. He or she took an oath before God, our friends, and family and swore to love me." That is a powerful thing. The best thing about marriage is the positive regard it gives you. It makes you feel special to know this person thinks that much of you. Infidelity destroys that image, sometimes forever. Think before you go there. Your relationship may never come back from it.

The Problem of Sacrifice

With all this self-centeredness going on, sacrifice is inevitably going to suffer. We don't believe that people are born just looking out for self. We believe this personality attribute is created. People are influenced by what is happening in their environments. The loss of sacrifice developed as a direct result of the changing world economy.

People could expect less from their government, so they needed to provide more for themselves. People had to develop ways to survive. For African Americans, who received little productive help from their government in the first place and suffered from great discrimination, this was especially devastating.

It is important to understand that we're not talking about selfishness. Selfishness is different from self-centeredness. Selfishness refers to a person feeling like he or she shouldn't have to share himself or herself, possessions, or time with someone else. Self-centeredness is a much different thing, specifically a more dangerous thing. Self-centeredness is more about being focused on strictly you. It isn't about sharing. In the case of selfishness, you are at least considering the other person and making a conscious decision to not share with him or her. When you're self-centered, the other person is not even in the equation. He or she doesn't even matter, and his or her feelings become invisible. The other person becomes an object that's in your way or a thing to be used as a means to get what you want. So, if everyone is walking around self-centered, you get a large contingent of individuals using and treating each other like objects, not recognizing each other's humanity.

In this condition, anything becomes possible. Huge R & B superstars can piss on little Black girls, and some people can overlook it. Black women can be domestically abused, and Black men can be thrown away like they don't matter in the criminal justice system. All this becomes possible when bodies are just relating to one another as objects. These are some obvious examples, but just think about some everyday ways we have become more self-centered. One example is brothers using sisters for sex. On the flip side, what about sisters who use brothers for their money? They are not really interested in the brother, but they like what his money can buy them. Both these scenarios cause pain and hurt. Self-centered people never think about the ramifications of their decisions on the individual they are dealing with or the larger society. Every time a brother hurts a sister, she carries that hurt with her into her next relationship. When we use each other as objects, our actions have a ripple effect in the wider community. This is not to say that people won't get hurt in a relationship. That is naïve. Of course they will. That is a part of love relationships. However, relationships require care and thoughtfulness. You must think about the feelings of the person you are relating to and see them like a person, not an object.

In this state, healthy African American relationships aren't possible because sacrifice has no meaning, and sacrifice is essential to love and developing a common purpose. In fact, some may see sacrifice as dumb and foolish. We have all heard people say, "Girl, don't work that hard for that man. He is going to leave you one day when he gets successful, and you will be alone. You better focus on yourself." Another good example is one of Akilah's friends who wants to get an advanced degree and needs her husband to work and take care of the finances of the house for a few years while she goes back to school. She feels that, if they sacrifice now financially, she can make more than enough money to help the family in the future. However, her husband is not supportive of her returning back to school, even if it means it would help the family in the future. His excuse is that he doesn't feel comfortable paying all the bills by himself. He doesn't feel like her dreams of going to get her advanced degree are worth the sacrifice he will have to make. But the real issue is that he fears she will become more educated and make more money than he does and leave him. He is scared and self-centered. He doesn't want to sacrifice.

Sacrifice is a commitment. It is about receiving as well as giving. This side is rarely talked about. If you know someone is sacrificing for you, it is your responsibility to uphold your end of the relationship. Akilah's friend needs to do her best when she returns to her education and finish as quickly and successfully as possible. She can't be tired or not care because people have altered their lives for her to achieve a personal and professional goal. Sacrifice is relational. People need to work together. When you are in a relationship with a self-centered person, growth and love become impossible because love is about sacrifice for the betterment of all involved.

The Meaning of Sacrifice

Sacrifice has very important meaning for a relationship. If you are looking for happiness in your long-term relationship, you must be willing to make sacrifices for its success. The maintenance of relationships requires sacrifice because sacrifice is linked to compromise, one of the most important aspects of a union. If you don't learn the power of compromise, you won't be in a relationship very long. Self-centered people don't know the meaning of sacrifice and compromise, which is why their relationships fail. What makes matters worse is that these people will blame the other person for the failure because they are self-centered, thus creating a vicious cycle.

People get confused because they think sacrifice costs them, but in actuality, sacrifice assists in the development of a strong relationship, which can help you reach your individual goals. If you talk to any successful person, one of the consistent themes you will hear from them, in addition to hard work and determination, is sacrifice. Tony Williamson wrote:

> Every successful person, every major accomplishment, every breathtaking achievement was FIRST made a reality by a sacrifice. So many wealthy and successful people today can point to a specific sacrifice they made, or a particular time period during which they deliberately endured hardship to achieve a goal. Great achievers, life's heroes and the super wealthy all share a common experience. They had to undergo a period so testing, so lonely, so difficult, it felt like death. But it was during that period of 'death' that their characters were fashioned.(Williamson, 2008)

It is no different for relationships. During times of sacrifice, relationship character is fashioned and developed. During this time, people in a relationship know they can depend on one another. Sacrifice is the key to relationship success and happiness. Are you being self-centered within your relationship? Or are you open to the sacrifice that is needed for your relationship to flourish?

Sacrifice and Common Purpose

The loss of sacrifice eventually results in the loss of common purpose. Sacrifice feeds common purpose. When a person knows you are willing to make sacrifices for the betterment of the union, he or she is more comfortable with joining his or her purpose to yours. This process is vital to healthy relationships because a relationship without purpose is like a ship without a rudder or oars. Furthermore, the relationship purpose must be common because competing purposes won't work either. Only competition and resentment will develop from competing purposes. Common purpose gives the relationship an origin or goal to return to when things feel like they are straying or veering off track. Through common purpose, people get a frame of reference by which to judge if situations occurring outside the couple should be tolerated or avoided. Essentially, common purpose gives a relationship meaning. Common purpose gives a relationship energy that would otherwise be unavailable and unattainable. The main problem relationships encounter regarding purpose is that they think the job is done once purpose is established. This couldn't be further from the truth. This is where sacrifice comes in. Sacrifice reaffirms purpose. It reassures everyone involved that the team is still on track and everyone is on board. Without signs of sacrifice, purpose dies. Without common purpose, the relationship eventually dies. Whether the relationship goal is a home, educational attainment, children, or business, common purpose is required to reach that goal and sacrifice is the prerequisite needed for common purpose to be established.

The post-Civil Rights era is a time that has severely tested Black relationships' level of sacrifice and common purpose. Unfortunately, it has been a time of "me" and "I." These stances are destroying Black relationships. We can't allow this current situation to corrupt our love for one another. It is through relationships with other positive and powerful people that we materialize what we what. If what you want is a powerful and beautiful union with another, then the importance of sacrifice and common purpose should be apparent.

Doin' Me

I don't understand this new generation.
They seem so damn selfish and lack real determination
for anything other than a dollar or big dreams of ballin'.
Don't ya'll have any aspirations that are noble or would be
considered a collective callin'?

Nope! It's all about money and then the ass.
Life is hard, complicated, and extremely fast.
I ain't got no time to be thinking about others.
You better focus on yourself 'cause you can't depend on your
so-called brothers.

Look, young'n, that's the point.
If you don't stop just looking out for yourself,
you ain't never going to individually rise to collect
your so-called wealth.

Look, old man, I must disagree.
In 2009, the slogan I live by is, "I must do me."

Now you see, young man, that's the type of thinking
we all fought against.
One day, you will see your do-me philosophy
will only leave you alone
on the wrong side of the fence.

CHAPTER EIGHT

BLACK MASKULINITY: THE PROBLEM OF PROPRIETY AND RESPONSIBILITY

"Till we have Black men in the seat of power, respected, feared, hated, and reverenced, our young men will never rise for the reason they will never look up."

Bishop Henry M. Turner

"There's nothing more dangerous and destructive in a household than a frustrated, oppressed Black man."

Nathan McCall

"We wear the masks."

Paul Lawrence Dunbar

Emotionally and psychologically turning Black men into Black boys is one of the by-products of living in American society. America has traditionally sought to marginalize and minimize African American males. One of the most destructive ways this is done is through the creation of characterizations and stereotypes. We learn in school and from our parents that stereotypes are beliefs that are unfounded and we shouldn't hold them because they are small-minded and simplistic in nature. While this may be true, it doesn't take away their impact on everyday life or stop us from at least mentally defaulting to them from time to time. Stereotypes are mental shortcuts that people use to make life easier and more manageable. Stereotypes develop over time from either exposure to or a popular-held narrative about a particular thing, group, or social activity. Contrary to popular belief, any social psychologist would tell you they are necessary in the right context. One can get out of a room because he has a stereotypical understanding of how a door works. I know not to walk down a darkly lit street at night because I know from movies, books, and other experiences that this might be a dangerous act. Unfortunately, stereotypes are not just relegated to things or situations, but they are often attributed to groups as well.

Often through historical discriminatory propaganda, certain group attributes are blown up and assigned to the entire group. After enough time goes by, the belief these attributes are characteristic of all members of the group become normal. So the academic achievement of some Asians over time becomes "All Asians are smart," or the rhythmic abilities of some African Americans becomes "All Blacks can dance." The problem with this process is that, if enough time goes by, the members of the group begin to believe the hype themselves and then begin to constrain and tailor their behavior to reflect these stereotypes. This can have very problematic outcomes for the group, especially if the stereotype is negative or limiting. No group in American society has been more stereotyped in a negative manner than Black men, and this has affected Black relationships in a very significant way.

Black men are categorized in various ways, many of which are negative. Scholars such as Joy Leary, Donna Franklin, and Claud Anderson have written extensively on the affects of the historical perception of African American males. From their analysis and our own observations, we have come up with the four most problematic stereotypical persona patterns of Black male behavior in America.

The Buck

Hyper masculine and testosterone personified describes the buck best. Everything that is stereotypically masculine is cool with the buck. Have you ever known a brother who is just too aggressive? You know, he's like Mike Tyson on steroids. That's the Buck. A fight? No problem. Sex with numerous, anonymous women? Cool. This is the cat who goes from zero to sixty in like five seconds. He escalates a problem from being a minor disagreement to a full-scale bar fight and acts like this is normal. Some may describe him as a thug who is down for whatever. This is a very problematic persona for a Black man to adopt because it predisposes him to being caught in the criminal justice system and/ or killed. It also makes multiple children with numerous partners likely. This type of behavior causes problems within a love relationship because the Buck always has drama and confusion occurring. He can be oppressive and misogynistic, if not downright abusive.

We see this persona illustrated in popular culture often. Some of the top selling Hip Hop artists exude this personality, mainly because it is a strategy to sell albums. In fact, many artists claim that, if you are not willing to wear the mask of hyper masculinity, you will not sell large quantities of albums and thus not be able to make a living doing your craft. Hyper masculinity sells big-time because America is comfortable with this image of Black masculinity. Think about some favorite Black movies, including *New Jack City*, *South Central*, *Menace II Society*, *Boyz n the Hood*, *New Jersey Drive*, and *Shaft*. All these movies have something in common. Many of the men in these movie exude aggression and use violence to solve problems. We are not saying these are not great movies, but they do subtly reinforce Black men in a particular image because the movie industry is not creating alternative images. Robert Townsend in *Hollywood Shuffle* tried to portray this dilemma that Black men find themselves in. In the movie, Townsend, an aspiring actor, tries to find parts that don't accentuate the stereotypes of African American men as robbers, pimps, and killers, but couldn't. So he decided to find work in a different field until he gets a dignified role. Many Black men are not bucks, but they are portrayed as such in popular culture. This image is why people clutch their pocketbook when they see a Black man walking on the same sidewalk or a clerk follows a Black male patron in a store. They are working off the negative stereotype that is so readily portrayed in movies and music.

This personality doesn't just develop in a vacuum. The buck was created because of the need for protection that the Black community craves. It is a defense mechanism. Instead of dealing with pain and hurt, it is easier and safer to portray hardness. How many times have we heard women say they need a thug or real man? This persona gives off a false sense of protection for women and the community.

The Nat

The Nat persona is named after Nat Turner, who led one of the most successful slave revolts in United States history. This personality type is associated with rebelliousness and opposition to oppression. Franklin wrote:

> Nat, the openly rebellious insurrectionist. He was the incorrigible runaway who, in the minds of whites, ravaged white women and attacked and killed other whites (Franklin, 2000).

The Nat is a brother who is down for the struggle. This strong Black man will protect the Black family and woman, and he would give his life, if necessary, for the African American community. This may sound like the ideal partner. For the most part, he is. But when does the war stop? The goal of any warrior or fighter is to put down his sword one day. The goal is peace, not perpetual struggle. This persona can sometimes use the struggle in an attempt to hide the sensitive and most vulnerable part of himself, his feelings. Nat sometimes brings the rebelliousness into the relationship as a distraction and to reaffirm his manhood, so the relationship becomes a proving ground that wears on and eventually kills the relationship.

Relationships are intimate and hard work. The Nat persona tends to not focus as much of his time on his feelings and nurturing his relationships as he does on defending them. There is so much work to do in the community, and relationships can become a distraction from the work of saving Black people. Men who possess this personality don't understand that the most important work you can do is family work. The great John Henrik Clarke said, "The family is the building blocks of the nation." Family is the foundation to any healthy and productive community. However, it doesn't happen in a meeting or rally. It happens at the dinner table with your children, in your bedroom with your wife, or in the living room with your family. That is the real work. This is not to say Nat shouldn't be in the community doing work on behalf of the Black community. He should! We need as many dedicated and talented people helping to uplift the African American community as we can get. However, your community work should never supersede your responsibility to your family.

The Sambo (Trickster)

Sambo is best known from Harriet Beecher Stowe's *Uncle Tom's Cabin*. He is associated with tricking and fooling people. For Sambo, survival depended on hiding his discontent from whites. Eventually, this survival trait evolved into the Sambo persona, which is about deception and hiding. It prevents others from knowing who the real you is. It is about fooling your partner. We have all seen *How to Be a Player* with Bell Bellamy, which portrays a young, successful African American man who consistently lies to women in order to have sex with them. This is just one of many movies that portray Black men as these players and womanizers. This persona and image is very destructive because it causes black women not to trust Black men.

This is not to say that there is a large portion of dishonest Black men out there. Unfortunately, the Sambo represents far too many African American men who are simply not being honest with their women. There are obvious problems associated with this personality trait. If you have ever been involved with a man who thought he was a player or pimp, was dishonest or deceptive, or hid his feelings for fear of getting hurt, the Sambo persona is probably what he was performing. The Sambo gets pleasure from the power of knowing he can successfully deceive his mate. This Sambo personality causes a lot of pain for his partner because the pain of realizing you didn't even know who your partner was can be devastating.

Stepin Fetchit

Stepin Fetchit was the stage name of Lincoln Theodore Monroe Andrew Perry, who created the Stepin Fetchit character as part of a vaudeville act. The character was meant to display a type of Black man who was dim-witted, lazy, and jive-talking. (Ironically, Perry was an educated and intelligent man who started out as a writer for the legendary *Chicago Defender*.) Perry did not develop the character to reflect all African American men, but, over time, because of the nature of America at the time, Stepin Fetchit became a personality persona that characterizes a Black man who is lazy and acts foolish or slow-witted. If you know a brother who always seems to underachieve or come up short, no matter how much support he has or a brother who never pulls his weight within the context of the relationship, then he is probably performing the Stepin Fetchit persona. Consider this example. A man is in between jobs, and he is chilling on the couch. His woman comes home from a long workday. No food is cooked, the house isn't cleaned, nor the dishes washed. This is the Stepin Fetchit personality. This personality is about fear. Stepin Fetchit uses laziness and underachievement to hide the fact he is afraid, specifically afraid of responsibility and greatness. The Stepin Fetchit personality kills the relationship by not doing his part, even though he is capable because, if he does his part, it will be expected he does his part regularly.

All these personas are made necessary by the social world of Black men. Black men exist in a racist and limiting society that often paints them as the society's ever-present and unsolvable problem. Oftentimes,

Black men reach for these personas as a way of coping and navigating safely through their social world and society.

The Problem of Propriety and Responsibility

Black women know the story all too well. They say it all the time. Brothers can't be sexually responsible. They don't respect Black women. They aren't taking care of their children. Basically, propriety and responsibility are suffering. Propriety can be defined as correct and appropriate behavior while responsibility is defined as the trait of being answerable to someone for something or being responsible for one's conduct in a certain situation. Both of these words are also synonymous with the definition of what it means to be a Black man or at least what Black manhood should mean. However, the aforementioned personas make it nearly impossible for Black men to act with propriety and in a responsible manner. All the personality traits highlighted in this chapter are about avoiding this level of manhood at all costs. The price of correct, productive, and proper manhood is propriety and responsibility.

The personas described previously are mainly about deception; deception cancels out propriety and responsibility. Propriety and responsibility can't coexist with deception. Therefore, Black men have to choose if they want to deceive or love Black women. Either Black men are going to be straight with Black women about their fears and pains that come from being Black and male in America or they are going to continue to disappoint Black women and reinforce the negative image that sisters have of brothers. Too many Black men have lost their belief in propriety and responsibility. They have allowed deception to become the Black man's greatest skill. Black men have hidden behind these personas for far too long and Black love has paid the price.

All these personas inhibit the building of strong and healthy relationships. These personas result in Black men pushing Black women further away. Relationships are a conscious process, and they take commitment and dedication. It doesn't just happen. When Black men push Black women away by adopting these personas, love is impossible.

Black Maskulinity (Failure, Guilt, and Fear)

The thing about this chapter that was so difficult is that Kamau had to reach deep inside himself and realize that, at different times in his life, he was each of these men. In fact, we think many brothers jump in and out of these personas, depending on the situation. So why do we still need these paralyzing personalities? How have they endured for so long? The answer to these questions can be found in three words: failure, guilt, and fear.

These personas have persisted for so long because of both structural and societal racism and Black men's feelings of failure, guilt, and fear. The previous chapters have been dedicated to capturing the level of pressure and obstacles that Black love has had to endure. We hope we have shown how pressure has been consistent on Black relationships. This has resulted in the necessity of Black men to wear masks as a way to hide feelings of failure, guilt, and fear. We call this process " Maskulinity." All of these personalities are used to hide behind. Black men who exude these personas are using them to escape these feelings and grasp some form of power in American society. However, Black love suffers in the process. The four preceding personalities are masks. They truly don't exist. The key for the community and Black men themselves is to get to the man behind the mask. The mask only drives a further wedge between Black men and women, ruins relationships, and hurts families. It's a lot easier to hide behind power and aggression than share feelings of inadequacy with your mate. It's easier to hide behind womanizing and deception than to work toward solving your pain and hurt with someone. It's much simpler to dodge responsibility and breadwinning by feigning laziness and underachievement. Yes, it's more convenient to be a revolutionary than to build a revolutionary love with someone. Love requires propriety and responsibility to your loved one. Masks hinder this process.

Masks are about politics, not love. They are used to plan, scheme, and manipulate situations and people. In the case of Black men, it is some sense of power and respect that the manipulation is done for. These masks that Black men wear have destroyed the dignity of Black relationships by reducing the relationship to the level of a game, as opposed to two people relating to one another and building something beautiful. Now it's a game, and you play or get played. This is the consequence of Black men wearing masks out of fear, guilt, and failure. Love is not a game. It is work, struggle, and persistence. There is no room for games. We need to take away the masks and restore Black Maskulinity back into something that is true and positive. Black men must face their fears and perceived shortcomings and rise to meet the challenges presented by contemporary American life with strength of character, intelligence and without masks. It's time for Black men to allow the world to see them for the true brilliant sons, fathers, and husbands they are. Only then can Black love and relationships prosper.

Trauma

Central to any discussion of contemporary African American males is the issue of trauma. We as a society are often very comfortable with discussing trauma as a contributing factor to self-destructive behavior when white women or white men are the topic. However, trauma is somehow disregarded when the conversation shifts to Black men, even though Black men are much more likely, regardless of income, to experience trauma than any other group. As a community, we cannot ignore the impact that incarceration, homicide, violence, racism, and discrimination has had on the psyches of our African American men and how it affects their attitudes and beliefs regarding marriage, love, relationships, and commitment. In many respects, the masks we discuss in the earlier part of this chapter become a coping mechanism for dealing with the trauma Black men have had to navigate and contend with in American society. They serve a protective purpose and become deeply ingrained in the psychology of some brothers.

Trauma can have both devastating and debilitating effects on its victims, and it can influence their behavior in many negative ways. What was once a rational and well-rounded individual can become a self-destructive enigma. A sister could believe she is in a relationship with a brother who has it together, but, in fact, she might be in a relationship with an individual who is suffering from the often-traumatic experience of being a Black man in America and whose negative behavior is an attempt to cope with that trauma. Many brothers are hurting and attempting to hide this fact from the women in their lives, and this is, in turn, destroying Black relationships. The trauma that Black men experience in the American context is undeniable and further discussion and research needs to occur regarding the consequence that trauma has on the romantic relationships of Black men.

Moving Forward (Black Men and Love)

This chapter focused a lot on what brothers are not doing correctly in relationships. For all of you out there reading and asking, "Do brothers do anything right when it comes to love and relationships?" Yes, of course. There are many brothers out there doing right by their wives and girlfriends, and we applaud them. However, we have some serious challenges going on between Black men and Black women, and we must begin the much-needed healing process. There are enough brothers out there not doing right to cause some of our relationships to be off balance and out of step. The work we have to do as a community must first begin with brothers stepping out of the negative roles that society assigned to them. Black manhood must be redefined. Roles that affirm who Black men truly are and promote balance and harmony within the Black family must be embraced and nurtured. Black manhood must support healthy Black unions between men and women. Black men have to begin feeling differently about themselves and their women and begin seeing Black women as partners and support systems. Healing begins with honesty and a commitment to change and growth. Brothers need to honestly communicate their feelings to themselves first and then to their mates. It is important for brothers to take off their masks and begin relearning who they are beyond the failure, guilt, and fear. Let's create the safe spaces in our relationships where this healing process can take place. Our relationships need to be a refuge from the harsh world, not by-products of it.

Our communities can't be healed without our brothers. We must begin to redefine Black manhood. We can't succumb to racism and white supremacy. We can't believe in and act out the negative images pushed upon Black men. It is time we toss those images and begin to create new ones that are more reflective of the Black manhood we wish to see.

Black Fatherhood

We would like to conclude this section by discussing the importance of Black fatherhood. As we are faced with the challenge of raising our son Jabari into a well adjusted man, we are often humbled by this herculean task. The pressure of this responsibility especially resonates with Kamau.

Being the product of a female headed single parent household himself, Kamau is extremely sensitive to how much Jabari needs him. Boys have a special connection to their fathers, and we firmly believe that the greatest problem facing the Black community today, other than incarceration, is the large percentage of our children growing up without the strong influence of their fathers in the home. By acting like they don't need a Black man for anything, including the rearing of children, some Black women are allowing Black men to get off the hook too easily. They are inadvertently cosigning Black male irresponsibility around fatherhood. If fathers are missing in action, they leave large voids in their children's lives in three major role areas: protector, mentor and provider. For these roles to be fulfilled, mothers and fathers must work together. While this can be challenging if there are hurt feelings or delinquent support, it is vital that fathers fulfill these roles.

Black men must take their role as protector of their children very seriously. It is important to understand that your children don't belong to you. They may have been born to you but they don't belong to you. They belong to the world. They are the gift of the future and as such require your protection until they are mature enough to fulfill their destiny or life mission. Imagine what the world would be like if Martin Luther King Jr. or Ben Carson were not protected. The world might have gone without their contribution and might look very different today. Unfortunately, children go unprotected too often, and thus our community and the world are robbed of their contribution. We are robbed by gangs, crime, violence, drugs and poor education. This must change. Black fathers must begin to protect the children again.

Fathers are often the first role model of masculinity a child sees. For boys, their fathers are often the blueprint for male behavior. For girls, their fathers usually are the measuring stick for future partners. It is very important that Black fathers know that their children are always watching them. They watch how you treat their mother and other women in your life. They watch how you handle conflict and money. They even watch how you express emotion and hurt. Black fathers must take the mentor role very seriously because what you say and do has power with your child and they carry it with them. Sometimes, they carry it permanently, so be careful and thoughtful when conducting interactions with your child present. Lead by example and be someone who your child can respect.

The last role is that of provider. Research shows that Black men take their role as provider more seriously than any other race of men and their masculinity is intricately tied to this role. Unfortunately, we live in a patriarchal and materialistic society, so for most Black men no money or adequate employment equals no masculinity and thus no participation in the family. The provider role is the role Black men struggle with the most. Most men feel that if they are not providing economic support they are not needed. What they (and some mothers) don't realize is that their presence is extremely significant even if they are struggling to make ends meet. Remember, your children are watching, and your participation in the family even as you go through the indignity of trying to scratch out a living makes a powerful statement. It says to your child "I'm here for you, no matter what." It also teaches your child to have strength, dignity and to uphold his or her responsibility even in the face of adversity. This is a valuable lesson.

Unfortunately, we fear that as long as the Black community and society continue to define manhood economically, the problem of Black men disengaging from the family may not change in the near future. Hopefully, we can get our arms around this problem as a community and restore Black men within the family, because despite what some say, they are needed.

Poem to the Brothers

How you doing Black man?
What's up with you disrespecting your biggest fan?

I am feeling like you don't love me,
like you don't recognize our beautiful unity.

I know you feel like you don't have much opportunity,
but, with our love, we can build any type of community.

I know this world consistently steals your possibility,
creates negative images of you,
and stunts your social mobility.

I feel sad when you allow the world to make you so crazy.

What's my loss, you may ask?
You focus on your struggles so much it appears you are
always looking for the greener grass.

I feel mad when you take your anger out on me.

What's the violation you may ask?
I feel I give 100 percent to you, and you just give half.

I feel scared about our relationship

What's the danger, you may ask?
That once we find each other, our love may not last.

I guess what I am trying to say brother is this.
It is not just your touch and kiss that I miss.

I long for your love and your strength in my life.
But, most of all, I miss being your wife.

CHAPTER NINE

No Woman, No Cry: The Problem of Faith and Proper Communication

"I have ploughed, and planted, and gathered into barns, and no man could head me! And ain't I a woman? I could work as much and eat as much as a man—when I could get it—and bear de lash as well! And ain't I a woman? I have borne thirteen children, and seen 'em mos' all sold off to slavery, and when I cried out with my mother's grief, none but Jesus heard me! And ain't I a woman?"

Sojourner Truth

Black woman listen/You ain't gotta cry no more/You ain't gotta cry no more.

Styles P, Hip-Hop artist

When it comes time to dish out the love and appreciation, it always seems like Black women are on the low end of the totem pole. They never seem to get the love they crave. If it's beauty, Black women are seen as lacking by society. If it's motherhood, Black women get stereotyped as poor caregivers. If it's business, Black women get paid and awarded less. Yep, being a Black women isn't easy, and it's been this way ever since Black people were forcibly migrated to this country. Black women have rarely had the luxury of the type of protection and adoration that white women receive. If anyone has a right to be angry and hurt, it is Black women. Unfortunately, this pain and anger is just as disastrous for Black love as the masks Black men wear to cope.

Anger, Resentment, Sadness, and the Problem of Faith

Many Black women have lost faith in love. This has occurred mainly because they have never known it in American society. The level of abuse Black women take from American society and masculine patriarchy has necessitated the loss of this faith. Love is something that many Black women are very skeptical of. If you mention love to some Black women, it's like you said a four-letter word because American society and the personas of Black men have so betrayed them. Black women have been lied to, beat on, hurt, abused, and left without much retribution or justice. This has caused many to harbor feelings of anger, resentment, and sadness toward love. Love becomes something that Black women lament as opposed to something they pursue or believe is possible. For many Black women, peaceful, powerful, and joyful Black love is more like a fairy tale than a reality. They either feel they have to accept some form of disrespect, settle for an unaffirming relationship, or not engage in the process at all.

The main thing we want to get across in these two chapters is that it is not the fault of Black men or Black women. We feel blaming gets nowhere but back to square one, that is, not realizing our full love potential. It's time for solutions, and part of the problem is the resentment, sadness, and anger that Black women are keeping inside them, which plays out in the form of their personas. Left unto themselves, these personalities would be somewhat problematic, but, when combined with the personas of Black men, things become extremely destructive. In the next section, we discuss the personas of Black women that have ensued because of the loss of faith.

Four Women

Nina Simone has a beautiful, often overlooked, song called "Four Women." It is an amazing journey into the psychological and historical shaping of Black woman. Nina really captures the pain and struggle of Black women as they attempt to transverse American society. From Nina's song, the brilliant scholarly work of Patricia Hill-Collins, Baba Wekesa Madzimoyo, and our own observations, we have outlined the four most problematic personas Black women have developed as protection from the pain, resentment, and sadness they feel.

The Jezebel

The Jezebel is the Black woman who is seen as the slut or harlot. She is the physically exploited and sexually aggressive Black woman. The Jezebel uses sex as a way of getting what she wants and hiding from the pain she feels. She believes there is power in this misguided sexuality. She says to herself, "If Black men want to over-sexualize me and use my body, then I'll give it to them and get mine in the process." We see this character a lot in popular culture, especially Hip Hop. It appears to be empowering, and some even tout it as New Age feminism. But there is no empowerment in this use of sexuality, only further resentment, anger, and pain as she realizes that, the longer this goes on, the deeper she falls into the Jezebel persona and the further she is alienated from herself. By fulfilling the fantasy of Black men, she only loses her own reality. The Jezebel persona comes from the societal narrative that Black women are promiscuous and loose, even though this couldn't be further from the truth. Black women are some of the most conservative women on the planet. This stereotype traps many Black women in a prison of their own sexuality. In this state, Black women become objects, and men treat them as such. They become labeled as the girls you don't marry and the women who won't raise your children, so most possibilities for strong and loving relationships with a man are cut off.

This Jezebel stereotype first came about on the slave plantations when slave owners justified raping and sexually exploiting Black women by labeling them loose. If Black women were seen as sexually irresponsible, then men could not be seen as accountable for abusing them. This type of thinking was sick and provided the rationale for Black women to be victimized.

Today, some Black women have to take back their sexuality and not allow anyone to exploit it. They must also deal with the pain and hurt they are trying cover up with the use of this persona.

The Matriarch

The matriarch (castrator) is the Black woman persona that is controlling and angry. Hill-Collins wrote:

> As overly aggressive, unfeminine women, Black matriarchs allegedly emasculate their lovers and husbands. These men, understandably, either desert their partners or refuse to marry the mothers of their children. (Collins, 1991)

These women are seen as always wanting to control the masculinity of their partner. These women rob themselves of the ability to relate to brothers in a real way. The matriarch hides behind her anger to avoid sensitive and vulnerable relations. For the matriarch, vulnerability is seen as a weakness, and she doesn't want to be weak. She feels Black women have been weak for too long. The controlling she does is an attempt to grab some semblance of power and determination over her environment. However, the matriarch only ends up pushing everyone away with her anger and insecurity, making relationships with Black men very difficult. By internalizing this stereotype, the matriarch only further alienates from herself and others.

The Strong Black Woman

The strong Black woman is like the matriarch in the sense she is trying to control her environment and believes women should personify strength. However, she defers in terms of how she deals with companionship. While matriarchs require men to push up against, strong Black women "can do bad all by themselves." They reject love and only seek men so they can tell them how much they don't need them. They are independent and need few. Black men are a burden to these women; relationships are viewed as unproductive. These women are so hurt that they hide behind independence, hoping this state will free them from their pain, but it never does. It only serves to feed their resentfulness. As more and more partners walk away from them, they tell themselves, "He couldn't deal with my strong, independent, and free nature." In reality, Black men can't deal with feeling like they are in a constant battle with their partner. It wasn't the independence. The wall drove him away. Love is cooperative work and requires collective struggle. It is not congruent with constant independence.

We hear sisters say, "He can't deal with me because of my strength," or "He is intimidated because I am successful and he is not." These types of attitudes only serve to push love away. These women sometimes use their status or material success to intimate and berate their partners.

The Mammy

Taken from the true-life African American women of the South during enslavement, the mammy persona is one where the Black woman plays the role of caretaker at her own expense. Certain Black women use this person to martyr themselves. The mammy often plays the guilt card with her man. Because she made inappropriate sacrifices for the relationship, she expects constant adoration, not payback. Unfortunately, this adoration is never adequate for two reasons.

1. She is rarely in an equitable relationship because she is so often exploited.
2. She feigns weakness and harmlessness as a way of receiving adoration, but no amount of praise is ever enough for her.

No amount of glorification will ever fill her emptiness or heal her sadness.

The mammy hopes the sacrifices she makes for her man will make up for all the pain and unfulfilled dreams she has, but they never do. She has an insatiable desire to be needed, but, no matter how much love she gets, she will always feel exploited and thus resentful. She will always make her partner feel guilty, eventually driving him away. The mammy is trapped in a prison of her own excessive selflessness and defacement.

The Problem of Proper Communication

In addition to the loss of faith that some Black women have developed because of the injustice they have received in American society, there has also been a loss of proper communication between them and Black men. This has mainly occurred because of the problem of personas speaking to one another. When one persona is speaking to another, you do not have two people talking. You have two scripts talking, complete with rules, regulations, and behaviors. The destructive scripts of some Black men and women have been conversing in America for centuries. Some want for these scripts to keep speaking. The job of the African American woman and man is to strip themselves of these personas and their accompanying scripts and relate to one another in a real manner. We have to move toward sincere relationships, which occur when people are connecting with their genuine and sincere selves and not script-laden personas. Sincere relationships assist proper communication by assuring that individuals are being real. People involved in sincere relationships are being authentic. The authenticity assists with proper communication by taking the guesswork out of interaction because you know that, no matter what is being said, it's sincere and connected to the speaker's true feelings. Sincere relationship communication comes from the heart of the person, not the defense mechanism he or she uses to protect himself or herself or the personality he or she has internalized to hide behind.

Any good counselor will tell you that communication is vital to having a proper relationship. Black women need to learn to communicate with Black men without the pain and hurt clouding the message. When the pain and hurt are prominent in the message, all brothers hear is the negativity and not what is important in the following message, "If you did this, it would please me." Black women must deal with the hurt and resentment they have; brothers must stop hurting sisters with impunity so we can heal these schisms between Black men and women and open up the communication again. We must put down the lies, deception, hurt, and pain and move toward having honest and sincere relationships. The movement toward a sincere relationship from an insincere one can occur in three steps:

1. Identify and discard any personas and accompanying scripts that are damaging the relationship. This means self-introspection is necessary.
2. Communicate true and authentic feelings regarding hurts, pain, sadness, fear, and anger. These feelings must then be discussed openly and honestly.
3. Make a commitment to do the work and struggle necessary to correct the situations causing the sadness, fears, and anger felt in the relationship. At the same time, make a pledge to develop strategies that will maintain and increase the joy, peace, and power within the relationship.

As a community, we must move toward creating and maintaining sincere Black relationships, along with increasing the communication power between Black men and women, so healing can begin.

Relationships are not a Proving Ground

Whenever the discussion in our home turns to relationships, Akilah's father can always be heard saying, "The white man may not give a Black man a job but he will always give the Black woman one." Black women, because of their unique history with white people, have always had more access in American society than Black men. During slavery, many Black women could be found working in the "big house," looking after the slave master's children. Some even were used as wet nurses (breastfeeding the slave master's children). This position gave Black women access to white society in a way that Black men couldn't obtain. When slavery ended, Black women were able to become nurses and teachers, while Black men remained laborers, for the most part. However, when Black men began to lose their jobs during post-fordism, Black women kept theirs because the industries they gravitated to were unaffected. Fields such as education, nursing and social services were dominated by Black women and shielded them from the shifting political economy. Once the manufacturing jobs left the urban areas, many Black men's employment opportunities left as well and thus Black men's status in the Black community declined.

What we have found when we speak with sisters is that they are frustrated and downright angry at brothers for not being successful. The truth of the matter is that all history is a current event; the problems brothers are experiencing today are linked to the oppression of yesterday. Too many times, we see sisters pass up great guys because he wasn't "perfect" or didn't have the right job. These are ridiculous reasons not to choose a partner considering our history in this country. The issues Black men face contemporarily are the responsibility of the entire Black community, not just brothers. We must hold our families together and tackle these problems as a community. Some Black women are missing out on great men because they are looking in the wrong places, looking at the wrong people, using faulty criteria to evaluate a person's spirit. We urge sisters to look past the superficial and deep into a person's spirit to find out what type of individual he is.

Some Black women are struggling with intellectual bullying. We can't tell you how many times we see sisters have to prove how smart and successful they are when they first meet a brother, often wearing it as a badge and letting it be known that they know their accomplishments will be a problem. This is especially true for some of our truly smart and accomplished sisters. The funny thing is, truth be told, Black men are not intimidated by the intellect or professional success of Black women. This is a huge misnomer that many buy into. For the most part, Black women who are educated have always gotten married more so than their less formally educated sisters. In fact, during the beginning of the 20th century, an educated Black woman would have several suitors competing for her attention. The fact is Black men want a Black woman who is cool and uses her intellect to better the relationship and not beat and intimidate him.

Both Black men and women have had an incredibly tough time in this country and neither one of us is doing that great when we look at our groups as a whole. However, Black women are outpacing brothers two to one in obtaining bachelor's degrees across U.S. college campuses and Black women are climbing the corporate ladder in unprecedented numbers. However, sisters shouldn't use that success to beat Black men up and remind them of their failures. Rather, we should all use our intellect and success to better our communities and families. We are not competitors but companions. We need to conquer issues that prevent us from being together, not strengthen the rifts between us.

It's Time

Sister, it's time you let go the anger and the pain.
It's time to heal the resentment and come in from the rain.

Please stop being holier than thou.
Maybe then we can take those sacred vows.

It is time to stop the accusations and the blame.
Yes, it's time for us to stop playing these games.

Oh, yeah, please stop saying, "I'm not on your level."
Because just a generation ago,
we were both still in the ghetto.
You act as if unlike you, I have no potential or mettle.

So you got some schooling and are on your perch,
and now this makes you think you can put me on the shelf?
Well, you look mighty lonely up there, all by yourself.

Please forgive my tone. I don't mean to be rude to you.
It's just that I fear I might be losing you, and
I don't know what to do.

If you took some time and stopped dogging me,
maybe you'd see
that you're just as much to blame for our breakup as me.

C'mon, girl, does your liberation really have to be
the cross by which I am crucified for the
whole damn world to see?

I know it seems like I'm wrong because I may call
you my shorty, jump off, honey, or boo,
but, if you read between the lines, you'd realize
I never stopped calling you!

CHAPTER TEN

THE LOVE ETHIC: A VISION FOR THE FUTURE BY RETURNING TO THE PAST

"There is no such thing as love in the beginning of a marriage. Love is a process of mutual growth of partners."
Kimbwandende Kia Bunseki Fu-Kiau

"An internal duality is externalized or elicited in the presence of a partner: what was half a person becomes one of a pair."
Marilyn Strathern

"God gives us anything we want at the price of work."
George C. Fraser

By now, you have probably realized the journey we wanted to take you on with this book. The goal was to look back into historical time periods and highlight how these major moments in African American history affected love. Then we wanted to look at where Black men and women are today, and we hope we accomplished both these tasks. However, with the final chapter, we wanted to bring everything together and answer the following questions. What is *The Love Ethic?* How can we make it meaningful again within the Black relationship?

We also wanted to highlight some of the pitfalls to this process and how to deal with them. We feel it is time for healing within the Black relationship, and there is no better place to start than now with this book. But first things first. What is The Love Ethic?

The Love Ethic

We mentioned the West African term "Sankofa" earlier. Loosely translated, it means, "Go back and fetch it." This is what we wanted to do with Black relationships. We wanted to go back and first analyze what has happened psychologically and sociologically between Black men and women. Next, we wanted to go back into our long and storied history as a people and retrieve a concept that speaks about how to guide love. We couldn't find any particular one that encompassed everything we felt love is. That's when we realized it. Love isn't one thing, term, or feeling. Love is a collection of emotions, feelings, behaviors, principles, and beliefs that require process and constant work. This is what the history said to us. African society was based upon this understanding. Love was the basis for all relationships, so there isn't one word, term, or concept. For our ancestors, love was a way of life. It permeated the entire family, community, and society. It was not just the feelings and fondness held by two people. Everyone in the community supported the union of a couple because everyone was responsible for the success of each couple. This was done for very practical reasons. Simply, communities and societies are made up of a collection of families. If the family suffers, then the community and society eventually suffers. We think that's where we are today. Because of all the historical racism that has happened to Black people, our families have taken quite a beating. We need to get back to loving and supporting one another. We need to embrace a Love Ethic, a guide for how to love one another. This book is an attempt to do that. Therefore, by using the process of Sankofa, we went back and combined valuable principles that we have learned are needed to create a successful, happy, and productive union. These principles form *The Love Ethic*.

The Love Ethic is comprised of thirteen principles or values: harmony, trust, balance, sacrifice, reciprocity, unity, justice, propriety, responsibility, faith, proper communication, common purpose, and order. These principles were chosen because we feel they best reflected the values of the African American experience and are essential to creating and maintaining happy relationships. They were also selected because we feel they are necessary for healing, and healing is what is needed at this time. At a time when the deep wounds of the past are coming to the forefront in our communities, we are ready for and in need of healing. At this time in our history, we must be open to love as a people. Caring and love surrounds us all, but they can't get through to some of us because of our pain. It is time to heal. We have never had this opportunity in America because of our struggle. However, we can no longer afford to hide from ourselves as a people because it is destroying our relationships. It is important to understand we are not hurting one another because we hate each other or are in a malicious mind-set. We are hurting one another because we are all walking around protecting our Collective Love Wounds (CLW) and hurt. We are not relating to each other. We are protecting ourselves from one another and hurting each other in the process. It is time to stop being so defensive with one another and open up to healing. We can only do this with each other, not in isolation. We must heal through our relationships. It is time to be aware of our CLWs and allow them to heal. When we are in denial of our CLWs, we subconsciously allow them to grow.

The following chart will outline each principle of *The Love Ethic*, indicate its importance, and show how it can heal Black relationships. Through *The Love Ethic*, Black couples can open up to the magnificent possibilities that Black love holds for their lives.

Love Ethic Principles	Why It's Important
Justice	Justice is about safety. It is meaningful because justice ensures that everyone in the relationship feels safe. If there is justice, then it means there is a dedication to fairness within the relationship. Justice provides a safe space for healing to be possible. If justice isn't prominent in the healing process, people will not open up for fear of being further wounded. A sense of justice is a prerequisite for any positive relationship.
Balance	Balance ensures you aren't living in the past or focused on the future at the expense of the present. Balance helps with focus. Balance provides the equilibrium that makes healing possible. Balance ensures no one person in the relationship is privileged over another.
Trust	Trust is about moving into the unknown with confidence and assurance. This can be done because you believe in the relationship. "I know this person won't intentionally hurt me." Trust helps with possibility. Healing is greatly related to possibilities. The very definition of healing is to take something that has been happening and change it. This is all about the possibility of what can be. Trust is essential in this process. Without trust, the miracle of healing can't happen. Without trust a productive relationship is just a fantasy.

Sacrifice	Sacrifice is related to the ability to delay gratification. Delayed gratification is closely related to achievement. So making a sacrifice in your relationship isn't about forgoing your needs for another. It's really about sacrificing now for the beauty to come. Healing is a seriously difficult process that requires work and commitment. It is not possible to heal without sacrifice. The most important healing sacrifice is the sacrifice of our ego. We often block our own happiness with our egos. Egos can be problematic within a relationship.
Reciprocity	Any relationship that isn't reciprocal is dead because it means that at least one of the members is selfish and not committed to the creation of a healthy union. Once reciprocity has left your relationship, the relationship is already over, whether you know it or not. Reciprocity is about accountability. If it is true what you put out comes back, this then becomes a way you hold people accountable for their actions. You become directly responsible for what you put in the world. Accountability is needed for proper healing to take place. A couple must hold each other accountable within the healing process. They must hold each other responsible for the energy they put into the relationship.
Harmony	Harmony is about connecting to the heart. Harmony allows one to come into the understanding of what he or she is feeling. Once you are in touch with your feelings, it becomes clearer what you want and need from an experience. This makes your next move more apparent. For healing, harmony is vital. Harmony brings understanding; understanding supports healing. It is through understanding that we heal. A large portion of healing is first understanding your wounds so you know how to heal them. You will need harmony in your life if your relationship is to succeed.

Unity	Unity is about cooperation and togetherness. Unity is necessary for any collective effort. Unity will be essential to your healing effort because your healing will take collective work. Without unity, any cooperative effort is just an empty promise.
Propriety	Propriety deals with proper behavior, but, essentially, it is conveying honesty. It takes a strong belief in honesty to act in the manner you know you should. Honesty is usually the first step to healing. Being honest with ourselves and our partner about our shortcomings, fears, and pain clears the path to healing. The first step is admitting the problem.
Responsibility	Responsibility relates to the concept of respect. When you act in a responsible manner regarding something or someone, you are explicitly saying you respect that thing or person. Respect is essential to healing because it is the ultimate devotion one can show to something. To want to heal a situation means you respect it enough to want to fix what's wrong.
Faith	Faith is about dedication. Having faith in something is to believe in it so much that you are dedicated to it, even in the presence of seemingly insurmountable odds. This is how we have to approach the healing of our relationships. We have to have faith in our families, communities, and relationships that they can change for the better. Without faith, healing is impossible.

Proper Communication	Proper communication speaks about feelings. In order to communicate well with someone in a productive manner, you have to be clear about your feelings. You have to be in touch with your feelings. If you are alienated from your feelings, then healthy communication becomes impossible. All you will accomplish is hurtful or deceptive communication, which solves nothing and definitely doesn't move you toward healing.
Common Purpose	Common purpose is linked to direction. If healing is moving your life in the proper direction, then common purpose means moving in that proper direction together, that is, being aligned toward a healing vision with another person. Common purpose takes various self-interests and combines them into a single, transformative force. Common purpose is important to community healing, our healing.
Order	Cards in a deck go in order. We count in order. The days of the week and months go in order, and our lives need to have order as well. In addition, the healing of our lives and relationships also has an order. We identify the problem, intervene in the problem, assess the intervention, and make changes to the plan if necessary so we can get it better next time. The entire universe is about order. Order is an imperative for healing because it provides structure. Without structure, healing is very difficult. If there isn't order in your life or relationship, it is very important you create some by discarding the habits, behaviors, and people who bring disorder to your life and relationships.

The Obstacles to Achieving Your Love Ethic

Whenever a person wants to make a positive change in his or her life, there are always pitfalls that he or she must be careful to avoid so his or her vision can come true. Creating a beneficial Love Ethic within your relationship is no different. There definitely can be deterrents to

Black relationships building a Love Ethic. Some of the possible obstacles are listed subsequently, along with strategies to counteract these negative influences.

1. People have a tendency to want and need to **cling to the past**. People incessantly carry around previous hurts and pain. No one's past is more painful in this country than that of Black people. The danger is that, when you cling to the past, you turn your back on the future. The past is gone. Any attempt to repeat, relieve, or lament is a sure way to get stuck in old patterns you have already outgrown. Clinging to past resentments and hurts will only create misery. We confront clinging to the past when we accept that healing is a **process**. The process of healing is a consistent one. A relationship is an ongoing thing, so the healing of it is an ongoing thing. As new challenges present themselves, healing after the challenge must take place. People don't fall in love in the beginning of a relationship and stay in love. It is a process to love one another, and there is no place for clinging to the past in the process. The healing process requires you let go of the past.

2. **Control** is about insecurity. People seek to control a situation when they are feeling threatened. Healing can be threatening because it means things that have not been working have to change. People often fall into patterns that are comfortable, even if they are negative patterns. When we put control in charge of our lives, we end up totally rigid. We do not allow for any spontaneity or vulnerability into our lives, and we stifle the creativity that is needed for healing. An effective way of countering control is to use openness. **Openness** provides the receptivity needed for healing to occur within a relationship. Openness ensures all parties are honest and ready for healing. Openness also increases your ability to listen and share, which are essential to healing. Being open

tells the universe, your partner, and yourself that you are ready for the miracle of healing.

3. **Laziness** breeds complacency. Laziness can fool us into thinking that everything is okay. Laziness can make us think where we stand presently is the final destination, but there are still places to explore, skies to fly, and healing needed to be done. All this requires work. **Work** is always necessary. Relationships never arrive at a destination. They are a constantly evolving entity that requires the same amount of dedicated work to maintain them that you put in to achieve them.

4. **Pessimism** destroys opportunities. When you are negative about the future, you intentionally shape the future. You disrupt the blessings that are there for you by not believing. Certainly, healing is not possible with a pessimistic attitude toward your relationship. The solution to pessimism is simple, hope. **Hope** provides a blueprint for the future. It allows people to construct the people and things they attract to them. There is a power in positive thinking. Positive people attract positive people and things. Therefore, a powerful and positive relationship will craft amazing possibilities for the future by facilitating healing today.

5. **Fighting** is about protecting yourself. It's like covering yourself in armor. The problem becomes that, in this protective stance, no one can get close to you. Your rage just pushes everyone away. A ferocious temper or simmering rage often hides a deep pain, a pain that needs to be protected. There is the belief that, if you frighten others away, you will prevent further pain and hurt from happening to you. However, the opposite thing usually happens. By covering and protecting our wounds, we only further deepen them and prevent them from being healed. It is time to stop fighting and have patience with yourself and others. **Patience** can prevent the fighting by helping people learn the importance of waiting to

see what happens. Everyone is not always there to hurt you. Give people a chance. People are always so quick to jump at one another as opposed to waiting, seeing, and then moving. Healing and forgiveness requires the ability to wait and be patient because these things don't happen overnight. Learn the importance of patience.

6. We are sometimes so busy trying to keep things together that we burn out and forget to rest. The process of healing is an arduous one, and it can exhaust one to a point where it seems meaningless to go on and continue. However, continue we must. We cannot allow **exhaustion** to lead to giving up. Black relationships are worth the work. They have produced people like Malcolm X, Martin Luther King Jr., Earl Graves, and Oprah Winfrey. Black relationships matter, and they can change the world, so we must turn to the principle of commitment. **Commitment** is about being dedicated to something so much that you are able to push through exhaustion. Commitment fights exhaustion and provides the rationale to continue. Commitment says, "This is important to do and must be completed." The healing of African American relationships is tough and serious work. Commitment is a must.

7. **Comparison** is about trying to be something you are not. It is about envying someone else's struggle or triumph because it brings him or her attention. There will always be someone more beautiful or successful than you and more needy and vulnerable than you. The key is not to judge yourself by others, but to see if you are fulfilling your own potential. The key for Black couples at this time is to not compare themselves to white, Latino, or Asian unions. It is to find their own level of success and strive for that. More importantly, Black men and women must not compare themselves to one another. No one's struggle is more difficult, traumatic, or imperative than another's. We are here together. We achieve

together. To guard against this, we need to have **compassion** with ourselves. We need to understand that America hasn't been very kind to Black love. Issues of employment, skin color, self-worth, beauty, and achievement have all impacted the Black relationship. We must have compassion for our reaction to these situations and obstacles. Compassion is a major part of healing. *The Love Ethic* is about loving yourself and your relationship enough to forgive yourself. Forgiveness is key to healing, and compassion is the first step toward it.

8. **Isolation** is used to stop pain. It hides the hurt we feel deep inside. We often fall into the trap of hiding our feelings from others and sometimes ourselves. This can cause us to become frozen or stuck in our pain. This frozen state prevents us from receiving and emitting warmth. The solution is to have **courage**, but not courage in the macho sense. It is in the sense to be brave enough to be soft. Only softness can melt the ice. Only softness can get you out of this frozen state and into a vulnerable position so love can flow again. Healing takes courage. The courage to heal yourself is vital to creating the relationship you want and the happiness you deserve.

The Love Ethic is about healing, seeing each other differently, and loving each other with a renewed vigor. Historical American oppression has shaped the way African American couples view love and behave toward each other. Now it is time to move toward healing. Until we heal as a whole, anything we create will turn to dust in our hands. A wise woman once told us that there are only two motivating factors in life: love and fear. She said a person usually acts because he or she loves something or fears something. Black people have been reacting out of fear for too long, that is, fear of what others might think, fear of consequences, fear of failure, fear of being exploited, and fear of being further hurt. It is time we switch to doing things out of love, that is, love of self, love of family, and love of relationships. We must heal our relationships not to achieve some form of progress, but to be complete again. This process will entail us viewing and thinking of each other differently.

We must have the courage to see each other with new loving warmth and act accordingly. Love is not a fairy tale. There are no Prince Charmings or beautiful, perfect princesses. It requires work throughout the process, but, if done correctly, you can find the best part of yourself in another. More than ever before, it is important that we see each other differently. Malcolm X said:

> We ourselves have to lift the level of our community, take our community to a higher level, make our own society beautiful so that we will be satisfied ... We've got to change our own minds about each other. We have to see each other with new eyes ... We have to come together with warmth.

Take the challenge and see one another with new eyes. Remember, as our close friend Malika Sanders always says, "We walk by faith, not by sight."

Thank you for reading and loving.

EPILOGUE

LIKE numerous Americans, we were extremely excited to usher in the Obama administration. Like many, we now have a renewed sense of hope for our future and look forward to the possibilities. One of the most exciting things about this new page in American history is the fact that a positive and dynamic Black family is on public display. Over the last few decades, we have heard so much negative publicity about dysfunctional, Black single-parent homes, including Black men not being sexually responsible or Black women not adequately understanding brothers. However, the world is now getting to see a new image of the Black family, one it usually doesn't get to see. It is one that has always been there. Barack and Michelle personify this image, which represents love, respect, and commitment. It suggests everything that is good about Black love. Barack and Michelle's love is a glaring example of what is possible when a couple commits to building and maintaining a Love Ethic with one another. So many of our friends and family have commented on how beautiful it is to see Barack and Michele loving and respecting each other. We agree! Far too often, this positive Black image doesn't get translated to the vast majority of Black people or larger society. The Obamas show the world and African Americans every day that Black love and family are alive and flourishing.

However, our one fear is that people will see the Obamas and think this type of relationship is beyond their reach or people might consider this type of relationship a fairy tale rather than something they can achieve in their own lives. In truth, love is promised to anyone who is willing to work to achieve it. The Obama's relationship should be an inspiration, not an anomaly. The Obamas represent what is possible when Black men and women work together and are committed to a larger vision. Great things can be achieved.

We hope this is the important gift you have received from this book. You have to do the necessary work in order to be in a healthy and loving relationship. They don't just happen. They require intentional thought and behavior. You get out of a relationship what both parties put into it. If one person puts great effort and another puts minimal, you'll get an uneven relationship filled with resentment and exploitation. If neither party puts work in, then you'll get fighting and a short-lived mess. However, if both parties put the work in, then you'll receive the magic that is a beautiful relationship.

Unfortunately, we recently heard a sister say that, because of the Obamas, she is now going to "step her relationship game up." We thought she was referring to being more introspective, committed, and responsible to her personal and relationship growth. However, this was not the case. She went on to say that now she is only going to date successful Black men and not waste her time with so-called scrubs. We knew then that she had missed the entire point of what Barack and Michelle's relationship represents. It represents two people who have done the necessary personal and professional work on themselves and their union to produce a healthy and loving relationship and family.

You can see that they are two people who truly enjoy being around one another. They look like they are good friends and genuinely like each other. When two people really enjoy each other's time and are great friends, you can feel the loving energy emanating off them. And you feel that with the Obamas. Enjoying spending time with the one you are with is a prerequisite for relationship success. Friendship, as Chuck D mentions in his foreward, is the foundation in which love rests.

The Obamas teach us that love is a journey, walked by two committed people who don't know exactly where they may end up but are committed to the quest nonetheless and not necessarily to the destination. We hope people will take this to heart as they proceed on their own love journey.

REFERENCES

A Great and Mighty Walk. DVD. Directed by S.C. Bourne. 1996. Black Dot Media.

Americans for Divorce Reform. "Divorce Statistics: Effects on Black Community." http://www.divorcereform.org/black.html (accessed September 10, 2008).

"America's Reconstruction: People and Politics after the Civil War." http://www.digitalhistory.uh.edu/reconstruction/section2/section2_09.html (accessed August 1, 2008).

Anderson, Claud. *PowerNomics: The National Plan to Empower Black America*. Bethesda: PowerNomics Corporation, 2001.

Ani, Marimba. *Let the Circle Be Unbroken: The Implications of African Spirituality in the Diaspora*. New York: Red See Press, 1994.

Armah, Ayi Kwei. *Two Thousand Seasons*. London: Heinemann, 1973.

Armah, Ayi Kwei. *The Healers*. London: Heinemann, 1978.

Blackman, L., O. Clayton, N. Glenn, L. Malone-Colon, and A. Roberts. 2005. The consequences of marriage for African Americans: a comprehensive literature review. *Institute for American Values*.

BNET Research Group. "The Shocking State of Black Marriage: Experts Say Many Will Never Get Married." http://find-articles.com/p/articles/mi_m1077/is_1_59/ai_110361377 (accessed February 10, 2008).

Collins. Patricia Hill. *Black Feminist Thought: Knowledge,*

Consciousness, and the Politics of Empowerment. New York: Routledge, 1991.

Franklin, Donna L. *What's Love Got to Do with It: Understanding the Healing the Rift Between Black Men and Women.* New York: Simon & Schuster, 2000.

Ginzburg, Ralph. *100 Years of Lynching.* Baltimore: Black Classic Press, 1996.

Hill, Shirley H. *Black Intimacies: A Gender Perspective on Families and Relationships.* California: Rowman & Littlefield, 2005.

Jessop, B. "Post-Fordism and the State." In *Post-Fordism: A Reader,* edited by A. Amin. Oxford: Blackwell, 1994.

Joseph, Peniel. *Waiting 'Til the Midnight Hour: A Narrative History of Black Power in America.* New York: Owl Books, 2007.

Kitwana, Bakari. *The Hip-Hop Generation: Young Blacks and the Crisis in African American Culture.* New York: Basic Civitas, 2003.

Kunjufu, Jawanza. *The Power, Passion and Pain of Black Love.* Chicago: African American Images, 1993.

Kunjufu, Jawanza. *Raising Black Boys.* Chicago: African America Images, 2007.

Kweli, T. *The Beautiful Struggle.* New York: Rawkus, 2004.

Leary, Joy Degruy. *Post Traumatic Slave Syndrome: America's Legacy of Enduring Injury and Healing.* Milwaukee, Ore.: Uptome Press, 2005.

Lemann, Nicholas. *The Promised Land: The Great Black Migration and How it Changed America.* 1st ed. Vintage Books, 1992.

Leon, F. Litwack. *Been in the Storm So Long: The Aftermath of Slavery.* New York: Vintage Books, 1979.

Loewen, James. *Sundown Town: A Hidden Dimension of American Racism.* New York: Touchstone, 2005.

Loewen, James. *Lies My Teacher Told Me: Everything Your*

American History Textbook Got Wrong. Revised and updated
edition. New York: Touchstone, 2008.

Mandara, J., and C. B. Murray. 2000. Effects of parental
marital status, income, and family formation on African
American adolescent self-esteem. *Journal of Family Psychology*
14:475–490.

Massey, D.S., and N.A. Denton. *American Apartheid: Segregation
and the Making of the Underclass.* Cambridge: Harvard
University Press, 1993.

Meltzer, Milton, ed. *In Their Own Words: A History of the
American Negro, 1619–1983.* New York: Thomas Y. Crowell,
1983.

Osofsky, Gilbert, ed. *Puttin' In on Ole Massa: The Slave Narratives
of Henry Bibb, William Wells Brown, and Soloman Northrup.*
New York: Harper & Row, 1969.

Prasad, Monica. *The Politics of Free Market: The Rise of
Neo-liberal Economics in Britain, France, Germany, and the
United States.* Chicago: University of Chicago Press, 2006.

Rawick, George P., ed. *The American Slave: A Composite
Autobiography.* Vol. 18. Westport, Conn.: Greenwood Press,
1972.

Some, Sobonfu. *The Spirit of Intimacy: Ancient African Teachings
in the Way of Relationships.* New York: Berkeley Hills Books,
1997.

Stack, Carol B. 1977. All our kin: strategies for survival in a
black community. *Journal of Black Studies* 8:117–120.

"The Importance of Sacrifice." http://www.jamaica-gleaner.com/
gleaner/20080507/news/news7.html (accessed on November
16, 2008).

The Inter University Consortium for Political and Social
Research, 1940–1980. Bureau of Justice Statistics,
1990–2000.

Tucker, B. M., and C. Mitchell-Kerman. *The Decline in*

Marriage among African Americans. New York: Russell Sage
Foundation, 1995.

United States Census Bureau. 2000. (June 2001) America's
Family and Living Arrangements: Population Characteristics.

United Stated Department of Justice. "Bureau of Justice Statistic
Bulletin. Prisoners in 2000." http://www.ojp.usdoj.gov/bjs/
pubalp2.htm#Prisoners (accessed December 12, 2008).

United States Government. "Homes and Communities." http://
www.hud.gov/offices/fheo/FHLaws/ (accessed December 2,
2008).

"War on Drugs." http://en.wikipedia.org/wiki/War_on_drugs
(accessed November 8, 2008).

Washington Post. "Marriage Is for White People." March 26,
2006, sec. B01.

Williams, Eric. *Capitalism and Slavery.* Chapel Hill: The
University of North Carolina Press, 1994.

Williamson, Tony. The importance of sacrifice. http://www.
jamaica-gleaner.com/gleaner/20080507/news/news7.html
(accessed December 5, 2008).

Wilson, William Julius. *When Work Disappears: The World of the
New Urban Poor.* New York: Vintage Books, 1997.

Zinn, Howard. *A People's History of the United States: 1492 to
Present.* New York: Harper Perennial Modern Classics, 2005.

ABOUT THE AUTHORS

KAMAU BUTLER, originally from New York City, has contributed over a decade of quality service delivery to various at-risk populations, including the homeless, mentally ill, incarcerated men, teens, and low-income families. Mr. Butler has worked extensively around the issues of training, nonprofit management, psychological assessment and testing, education, and vocational development. Labeled at-risk and low-achieving and told he would be nothing more than a gang leader by his high school guidance counselor, Kamau now holds an associate's degree in mental health and human services and a bachelor's degree in psychology from Hunter College. In 2004, he received his master's degree in social work from Clark Atlanta University.

Currently, Kamau is completing his PhD in social service administration from one of the most prestigious educational institutions in the country, the University of Chicago. He has gone from the streets of Brooklyn, New York, to the halls of an elite university, which blesses him with a unique perspective not commonly found in academia. Kamau's research interests are centered on various issues that affect African American families and males, such as Hip- Hop, Black male incarceration, Black marriage, and public education.

AKILAH   WATKINS-BUTLER

has spent the bulk of her professional career and life improving the conditions of at-risk children and communities. In 1991, at the age of thirteen, Mrs. Watkins-Butler founded I AM Corporation, a nonprofit organization dedicated to helping low-achieving youth self-actualize. By will, determination, and skill, Akilah built I AM's annual budget to well over $400,000.

Akilah has been featured in *Black Enterprise, Ms. Magazine, Essence*, and the *New York Times* for her outstanding community work. In addition, she has received the Oscars of Youth Activism, the Do Something Brick Award (1998), and an Essence Award (2001) for her accomplishments. Akilah has been featured on numerous television broadcasts, such as CNN and Good Day Atlanta. Moreover, Akilah represented the United States in 1995 during the 4th World Women's Conference in Beijing, China and, in 2000, during the National Activist International Exchange program in Johannesburg, South Africa.

Mrs. Watkins-Butler earned her undergraduate degree at Empire State College in community and human services. Also, she is an alum of Southern New Hampshire University, earning two master's degrees in community economic development and business education. Presently, Mrs. Watkins-Butler attends the University of Illinois, where she is completing a PhD in sociology.